MW00397548

More Stories from **Guideposts:** *Friendship at Its Best*

MORE STORIES
from
Guideposts®

Friendship at Its Best

Tyndale House Publishers, Inc.   Wheaton, Illinois

Guideposts is a registered trademark of Guideposts Associates, Inc.

Library of Congress Catalog Card Number 91-65398
ISBN 0-8423-4560-4
Copyright © 1991 by Guideposts Associates, Inc.
All rights reserved

97 96 95 94 93 92
8   7   6   5   4   3   2   1

Contents

Part One

Friendships
That Win
Enemies

We were a happy group, except for the
woman who gave me . . .

The Silent Treatment

BY LOUISE MAJORS
WESTMINSTER, CALIFORNIA

The summer of 1953, before our children went off to elementary school, I started looking for a job. I pounded the pavement unsuccessfully for weeks. Then I answered an ad placed in the *Los Angeles Times* by the California Institute of Technology.

The opening turned out to be for an accounting clerk at the Cooperative Wind Tunnel facility, which tested aircraft parts for strength and wind resistance. Carl Jorgensen, who headed the finance department, was a matter-of-fact man who peered kindly through his black-rimmed eyeglasses and said, "Louise, you have excellent qualifications. If you are willing to start at minimum wage, a dollar and nineteen cents an hour, you can begin next Monday."

I gulped. In my previous job, before I took years off to rear our children to school age, I'd made in a day almost as much as he was offering for a week. But I'd already been turned down for six other jobs. "Thank you, Mr. Jorgensen," I replied. "I want the job very much."

Come Monday morning I went directly to Carl Jorgensen's office. His cheeriness put me at ease, and I followed him as he introduced me to the office staff. "Everyone here goes by first names," he said. He stopped at the first desk. "Hildur is our payroll clerk. Hildur, this is Louise, our new accounting clerk."

I smiled, "I'm glad to meet you, Hildur."

She was grandmotherly with soft, wavy white hair, rimless eyeglasses, smooth fair complexion—pleasant looking. She looked me up and down, then her expression changed. Getting up, she railed, "We don't need an accounting clerk. I don't know why you were hired!" She slammed shut the record book she'd been posting, snatched up her purse, and stomped out the door.

Everyone's mouth dropped open. I stood stupefied, feeling the blood surge to my neck and face. This was awful!

Carl Jorgensen was quick to regain his composure and started more introductions: "Bernice, Manna, and Esther—the last desk on the right—are members of the steno pool. Joy is our mail clerk and relief switchboard-operator. Please welcome Louise."

It didn't take long to be welcomed. The "girls" (as even we called ourselves back in the '40s and '50s) were very kind and helpful, and they asked me to have lunch with them later.

I'd just returned from Carl's office with my first assignment when Hildur reappeared. She ignored everyone, slammed drawers, and was testy on the telephone and to people stopping at her desk. There was no conversation in the office until shortly before noon.

"Did you bring your lunch today, Hildur?" Bernice asked.

Hildur looked up warily. "Is *she* going to lunch with you?"

"Yes."

"I'm working," Hildur snapped.

I liked the "girls"; they were relaxed and friendly. But I was troubled by Hildur. On the way back to the office, I mentioned I was going to bring my lunch and study in my car, starting tomorrow. I didn't want to be the reason for Hildur not eating with the others. She would soften up after a bit, I reckoned.

Meantime, I was enjoying the bustle of the Wind Tunnel facility—"the Tunnel" as we called it. Four or five times a day the warning bells would go off, and we'd hear the high whine of the turbines that generated the air flow in the test chamber. I loved the family atmosphere in the halls and offices. No matter whether you were greeting a hard hat or a world-famous scientist, it was "Hi, Ted" or "Hi, Fred," with a genuine friendliness and a shared sense of mission.

Yet Hildur didn't mellow. Weeks passed, and the tension only worsened. When I was out of the office, the "girls" said Hildur was congenial and talkative. The minute I walked in, she fell glaringly silent. Each morning she would ignore my cheery greeting.

I searched my Bible and ended up by pasting my mother's favorite Scripture in my middle desk drawer. As Hildur rebuffed each of my advances, I referred to it: "Bless them that curse you, do good to them that hate you, and pray for them which despitefully use you" (Matthew 5:44). I nearly wore out that drawer as the weeks went by.

A couple of months passed. One of the women I'd come to know in the next office was retiring. We all chipped in for a little afternoon send-off party that I was looking forward to. Maybe I could get an opportunity to talk with Hildur in this kind of a setting.

I was just getting ready to go when Bernice called over to Hildur, "Aren't you going to the party?"

Hildur glared over at me, then at Bernice. "Is *she* going?"

"Well, of course," Bernice said, "we're all going."

"Then I'm not."

I gritted my teeth and then said as evenly as I could, "Oh, Bernice, you all go on without me. I've got some catching up to do. Maybe I'll come in later."

But after they'd gone, I brooded. I pulled open my drawer, and there was the message. "Do good to them that hate you," I read aloud. Then I said, "Lord, You know I'm doing that. My question is: How long must this go on?"

As if by answer, I recalled a scene of twenty years before, when I'd had a falling-out with an adolescent friend. I was back in Mother's kitchen and she was telling me, "Seventy times seven, that's how often Jesus told us to forgive. Remember, Louise, the only way to destroy an enemy is to make a friend of him."

I shut my drawer gently. "Thank you, Lord," I whispered.

A couple of months later, on a windy March day, we had a torrential rainstorm. Creeping along in our old green Pontiac coupe on my way home, windshield wipers batting furiously, I spotted Hildur standing at a bus stop, huddled under an umbrella. I stopped and flipped open the passenger door.

As kindly and firmly as I could, I said, "Hildur, get in." She hesitated a second and then lowered her umbrella and scrambled in. Water dripped from her hair and she looked soaked through. I turned up the heat. "Hildur, please give me directions as we go," I asked.

Except for directions, she was silent all the way to her apartment in East Pasadena. Before dropping her off, I asked her if there was anything I could do. She said, "No, but thank you very much."

After I had watched her disappear into her apartment, I exulted, "Well, praise the Lord, at least she talked to me!" All the way home I felt elated, singing the old hymn "Love Lifted Me." Hildur may not have changed, but at last *I* felt better.

The next morning was bright, crisp and clear. "Good morning, Hildur!" I said when I got to the office.

"Good morning, Louise," Hildur said with a shy smile. The

whole office seemed to give a collective sigh of relief. The harmony was instant; it was as if someone had let the sunshine and singing birds right into the office.

That Friday Hildur and I went out to lunch. She admitted her job was her love, and that she had felt threatened when I was hired. She thought management intended to replace her with me. But over lunch we became friends.

On the way home from work I stopped in Pasadena, had my hair cut and styled, bought a geranium-red dress, patent leather shoes with a pocketbook that matched, and a nifty wide-brimmed straw hat.

Mac and the kids went into shock when the "new me" walked in that night. "Wow," Mac said, "I thought your job was getting you down!"

"That was last week," I said. "Now it's getting me up!"

And it stayed that way. Making a friend of Hildur was one of the hardest things I ever did, yet one of the most rewarding. It was wonderful to have her as a friend. I have Jesus to thank for that.

Mama's Plan

BY MARION BOND WEST
STILLWATER, OKLAHOMA

*Mildred—she was always there waiting
for me after school. And I was terrified.*

I suppose it was the reality of my first grandchild, Jamie, starting school that triggered the bittersweet memories of my first year of school. The year was 1942. "Miss Edna" was that marvelous old-fashioned kind of teacher who gladly put her entire life into teaching. I loved school: the smell of chalk and color crayons; the way the old wooden floors smelled after Jim, the janitor, had waxed them; and having my own desk that was just my size. There was, however, one overwhelming problem with school. Mildred.*

Daily when I walked the short distance home after school, Mildred would taunt me, hit me, and scare me. I was absolutely terrified of her. She had failed first grade and was a year older than I. Mildred didn't have any friends, so she seemed to concentrate on making enemies. Because I was one of the smallest children in first grade, she had selected me as her number one enemy.

As we walked home after school she would continuously step on the back of the heels of my shoes and cause the shoes to slide down. Then, when I stopped to adjust them, Mildred would slap me hard on the back. As soon as the dismissal bell rang each day, my heart started to pound and I blinked fast so I wouldn't cry.

*Name has been changed.

9

Pretty soon my mother figured out something was wrong at school. I didn't want to tell her about Mildred. I sat close to the radio listening to *The Lone Ranger,* pretending not to hear her questions about school. Mother continued to question me, and finally I sobbed out the whole story. "You can't do anything, Mama. *You can't.* Everyone will think I'm a baby."

It was impossible for Mother to pick me up after school. She had to work. My father had died a few years earlier. I didn't have any sisters or brothers to watch after me. I couldn't imagine what my mother might do. I was certain there was no answer—no answer at all for a problem this big.

The next day at school, Miss Edna leaned over my desk and whispered, "Marion, dear, could you stay after school and help me with a project? I spoke with your mother last evening and she said it would be fine with her." Her blue eyes were understanding and she smelled like Jergens hand lotion. I decided right then that all angels must have blue eyes and smell like Jergens hand lotion. I nodded eagerly.

I remained joyfully at my desk when the dismissal bell rang. Mildred looked confused for a bit, but filed out with the others. After a while Miss Edna said that I'd better be going on home. She stood on the front step of the school and waved to me. I skipped up the hill without any fear whatsoever. Then, just as I got to the top of the hill, I heard familiar footsteps behind me. Mildred had waited for me. She immediately stepped on the back of my shoe and slapped my back. I cried. I couldn't help it.

When my mother saw my face after she got home from work, she questioned me. I begged not to go to school and I didn't sleep much that night. The next morning she said, "Marion, I'm going to walk up the hill with you today. I believe we'll see Mildred." Mildred walked from way across town to school. She never bothered me on the way to school, only afterward.

"Oh, Mama, please don't do that! Don't say anything to Mildred. It will just make her mad. Let me stay home by myself. Please, Mama."

"Hurry and get dressed, Marion." Her voice was gentle, but quite firm.

"Ple-e-ease, Mama."

"Trust me, Marion. I have a plan." My insides were in turmoil. Why couldn't my mother understand that no plan she had dreamed up was going to work? We bundled up against the bitter cold and started walking up the hill. Maybe we wouldn't see Mildred, I hoped. But my mother had this confident look. I knew the look well, and I had a sinking feeling that we would see Mildred and that Mother would use her "plan."

Sure enough, just as we got to the top of the hill and I had to go in one direction to school and my mother in the opposite direction to her job at the bank, but we spotted Mildred. We waited a few horrible moments as she approached us. She pretended not to see us, recognizing that I had my mother with me.

"Hello, Mildred," Mother said quietly. Mildred stopped, frozen as still as a statue. Her hands and face were bright red from the intense cold. Her oversized coat hung open. There were only two buttons on it. The rest were missing. Underneath she wore a cotton dress, as though it were summer. I was so wrapped up I could hardly walk. I even had to wear undershirts.

Mother stooped down to Mildred's level. She didn't say anything at first. Instead she rapidly buttoned Mildred's coat and turned the collar up around her neck. Then she fastened back this stubborn piece of hair that forever hung in Mildred's face. I stood off to one side watching our breath linger in front of our faces in the frigid morning air, praying that no students would happen by and that my mother's plan would be over quickly.

"I'm Marion's mother. I need your help, Mildred." Mildred looked intently at my mother with an expression I couldn't identify. Their faces were inches apart. My mother's gloved hands held Mildred's cold ones as she spoke. "Marion doesn't have any brothers or sisters. She sort of needs a special best friend at school. Someone to walk up the hill with her after school. You look like you'd be a fine friend for her. Would you be Marion's friend, Mildred?" Mildred chewed on her bottom lip, blinking all the time, and then nodded.

"Oh, thank you!" Mama said with certain confidence and gratitude. "I just know you are someone I can depend on." Then she hugged Mildred long and hard. She gave me a quick hug and called to us as though nothing unusual had happened. "Bye, girls. Have a good day." Mildred and I walked on to school, stiffly, like mechanical dolls, both staring straight ahead without speaking. Once I cut my eyes over her way. Mildred was smiling! I'd never seen her smile before.

We walked up the hill each day after school together, and pretty soon we were talking, laughing, and sharing secrets. Mildred started tying her hair back the way Mama had. Sometimes she even wore a hair ribbon. Someone sewed buttons on her coat, and she buttoned all of them and always wore the collar turned up. Somehow I started calling her "Mil." Then others did too, even Miss Edna.

"Hey, Mil, sit by me," someone called out at lunch. "No, Mil, sit with us," someone else begged. Mildred shot them a happy smile, but she always sat with me at lunch. My mother usually included something in my lunch especially for Mil—even notes of gratitude. Mil always let me get in front of her in the line at the water fountain.

Valentine's Day was a very important event in first grade back in the '40s. We made huge valentine boxes and set them on our desk for a valentine exchange. I pulled out an enormous valentine toward the end of the party. Everyone stood up to see better. It was store-bought! And had obviously cost a lot. Most everyone had made their valentines from red construction paper, lace, and glue. Ahhhs and ohhhs floated out over the classroom and seemed to linger, suspended in the air, as I opened the magnificent valentine. Printed neatly in bold red letters inside the card was: "From your best friend."

I looked over at Mil. She was sitting with her hands folded on top of her desk and smiling the biggest smile ever. She had a red ribbon in her hair. Mildred smiled a lot now. She was getting good grades now too and didn't stuff her papers inside her desk anymore. Her eyes darted over and met mine. Right then I knew my mother's plan had worked.

I didn't understand Mama's plan back in 1942, or for years afterward. But along the way I discovered where my mother had got her remarkable plan. And I've learned that the plan works in all kinds of impossible situations: "Love is patient . . . kind . . . does not act unbecomingly, . . . is not provoked, does not take into account a wrong suffered . . . believes all things, hopes all things, endures all things. Love never fails (1 Corinthians 13:4-5, 7-8).

The Cop

BY WAYNE BARTON
BOCA RATON, FLORIDA

He was a son of the projects too,
but that didn't make him welcome
on these tough streets.

We don't want that cop round here anymore!" The deep, angry voice rose from the back of the packed community center of the Dixie Manor housing project in Boca Raton. The room was crowded with sullen-faced residents. They'd called an emergency tenants' meeting, and there was only one item on the agenda that sticky, sultry night: me.

"Yeah," came a second voice from a cloud of cigarette smoke, "he causes more problems than he solves!"

Where have I gone wrong? I think of myself as a good cop. The police department had assigned me this difficult beat in the Pearl City section. It's a rough neighborhood, and the residents, some of whom had grown to see the police as the enemy, had asked for a cop who understood them. Everyone agreed that I was the right cop for the job, and I thought I'd been doing my job prowling the dismal, decaying streets in my big blue-and-white police cruiser, busting corner drug peddlers and muggers who preyed on Dixie Manor.

"Things are worse since he got here," chimed in a young mother holding a squirming, gurgling infant and pointing at me. "The dopers take it out on us. We were better off before."

It made me so angry to hear such talk that I wanted to quit

on the spot, go somewhere where my work was appreciated. But there was truth in what she said. These people were scared, and I scared them as much as the criminals. I came and went, but they had to live here. What upset me most, though, was that these were my people.

You see, I am a son of the projects, and I'll never forget what it was like growing up in that environment. Though ours was a serious, religious family, I still lost two older brothers to the streets. I can remember going to visit them in jail with Mom and Dad on Sundays after church. I hated those visits—the smell, the loud noises, the glaring light—everything about jail made me sick. But that's where something changed me.

One Sunday when I was about twelve, my folks were talking to my oldest brother in a dim corner of the visiting room. Bored and restless, I wandered over to a window. I could see prisoners, most of them young and black, milling aimlessly in the yard below. Except for the walls and uniforms, this could have been any street corner near my block. I even recognized some faces.

"What's up, kid?" A voice had interrupted my brooding. I turned and saw a policeman looking me up and down.

"Don't like this place," I answered sourly.

"Good." He grinned. "You're not supposed to."

I returned my gaze to the yard. What was this cop's angle? I wondered. Why was he bothering with me? I hadn't done anything wrong—yet. But was I fated to end up walking that yard like so many others from my neighborhood?

I saw him again a few weeks later. The cop sat down next to me on a bench and started shooting the breeze. I kept my distance. After all, he was a cop, the enemy. But on those Sunday visits, the cop would talk to me about his work on the streets cracking cases, rescuing people, putting crooks in jail, helping find lost kids. All of a sudden one day, I left that jail knowing what I wanted to be.

"You know something, Mom?" I said that night at home. "I want to be a cop."

For a moment Mom just stared at me. I didn't know if she was mad or if she was going to cry. But then she smiled. "Oh, Wayne," she said. "It would be an answer to my prayers to have just one of my boys on the right side of the law. *On God's side.* You hang on to that dream, Wayne."

It wasn't an easy dream to keep. I saw friends and classmates falling into crime and going to jail. I was jeered at sometimes, cut off for attending church and working in school. But I made it to the police academy, and when I got a chance to work in Dixie Manor, I thought I could really make a difference, do good in a neighborhood that needed a cop who understood them.

Now, feeling very much alone in this seething crowd, I couldn't figure out what had gone wrong. I thought I was *supposed* to be an aggressive cop. Maybe I was too good. I was about to throw in the towel when a firm voice came from the front row. "What's *wrong* with you people? Have you given up?"

I saw Mrs. Jackson standing up, a stately figure, tall and white-haired, with a rich voice that carried enough authority to quiet the room. She'd been one of the few to greet me when I came to Dixie Manor. She'd stopped my patrol car and presented me with a plate of homemade buttermilk brownies. "Welcome," she'd said simply. It was about the only time I *had* felt welcome.

"Have you folks all gone crazy?" she continued. "We need a man like Wayne Barton, someone who's not afraid to stand up to the dopers and thieves, someone who knows what the streets are about. Think of your families and kids. Are we going

17

to surrender our neighborhood, our home?"

There was an uneasy silence, then more discussion. Finally it was agreed—more out of respect for the venerable Mrs. Jackson than for me—that I would get a reprieve. The community board would not request that I be transferred off the Dixie Manor beat. When the meeting adjourned I edged my way through the crowd.

"I want to thank you, Mrs. Jackson—"

"Listen here, Wayne," she interrupted somewhat sternly. "Now that you'll be with us a while longer, maybe it would be smart of you to get out of that tank of yours and start patrolling on foot. Get to know us a little better, loosen up, meet some of our *good* people. They're out there, you know."

Her reprimand stung. I spent the rest of the night brooding about what she'd said. Was there something to my job that I was missing? Out of desperation I vowed to give her suggestion a try.

Patrolling on foot didn't bring any immediate results. People still turned their backs or looked right through me.

But then there was Jenny, a little neighborhood girl I'd often seen playing in the dirt. One time I'd waved from my patrol car and rolled down the window. "And how are you today?" I'd asked with a smile.

Jenny had just opened her mouth to answer when a shrill cry from behind made her jump. "Jenny, get away from that cop!" It was the girl's mother. Jenny ran off.

On foot patrol I saw Jenny again. I noticed her mother spying warily from a window, but this time she didn't interfere. Jenny and I had a nice little talk.

That got me thinking about the cop who'd first taken an interest in me. Here was a cop who was as interested in a good kid as in a bad one. He'd reached out. What lesson could I learn from that? "Get to know us better," Mrs. Jackson had said. *Maybe I need to do some reaching out.*

I started with the kids. I greeted every one who crossed my path. I learned their names and talked with them the way that cop had talked to me. I showed them that I could be a friend, not an enemy. "Call me Wayne," I said.

An amazing thing happened in Dixie Manor. A friendly gang of fifty or so curious kids began following me on my daily beat, asking me questions about my work, watching how I handled myself. I'd think up things we could do. One day I had them pick up trash along the sidewalk, promising a prize to whoever picked up the most. We really got the street looking sharp! Then came the supreme compliment: A couple of kids said they'd be interested in doing police work when they grew up. I felt like the Pied Piper.

Still, older kids and adults viewed me with suspicion. And I continued arresting druggies and thugs. That didn't stop. But slowly folks warmed up: an offer of something cold to drink on a hot day, a flickering smile from a mother with her young'uns, and an occasional "How you doin' today, Wayne?"

Now, litter collection may not sound like gang busting, Elliot Ness–style crime fighting, but I was realizing that if these folks wanted to take back the streets from muggers and push-ers, then the streets would have to be the type they'd want back. The neighborhood was a mess: shattered glass every-where, bottles, cans, derelict cars where crack addicts lurked, debris of every description. Mrs. Jackson agreed that an organ-ized cleanup sounded like a fine idea. I got the word out to the kids. We'd make a real event of it.

Early one Saturday, I headed a caravan of city dumpsters, vans, tow trucks and cars full of outside volunteers onto the streets of Dixie Manor. Politicians, lawyers, city managers, doctors, secretaries, the press, the chief of police, even the mayor—had all given their day off to this project.

When we arrived, not a soul from Dixie Manor was there to greet us. I was crestfallen. I'd been talking this day up to the kids for a couple of weeks. "Well," I said trying to sound jaunty, "let's just get started without them."

As we began our cleanup, hauling and sweeping and hosing, I detected a few skeptical heads poking out from windows. Some locals driving by pointed in disbelief. But we just kept working in the hot Florida sun. I was going to show them I meant business, that I could be as tough about trash as I was about crooks. Finally a young voice rang out from a top floor, "Yo, Wayne! What's up?"

"Man, it's cleanup day, remember? Get yourself down here! And make sure to check with your mama first."

A minute later the boy and his older brother walked outside rolling up their sleeves. Then more kids came, some still snapping their jeans closed or pulling T-shirts over their heads. And as we worked, first one, then another, then more of their parents pulled rakes from under their porches or brooms from their kitchens. It seemed like all of Dixie Manor was out, neighbors laughing and visiting like they hadn't seen each other in years!

I saw little Jenny dragging a bulging garbage bag. By her side was her mother, who gave me a smile and a wave. And there was Mrs. Jackson, giving encouragement. *Get to know us better, Wayne.*

That day we sent away seven truck loads of trash and hauled off twice as many junked cars. The transformation was a miracle to see. But the change in the residents was even greater. I saw them smiling. No one was cowering behind barricaded doors. Good people were taking a stand where it counted: in the streets. Dixie Manor had changed a little bit, and so had I.

Sometimes the long arm of the law must reach out and embrace as well as collar. I learned that as a boy visiting my brother in jail, and Mrs. Jackson and Dixie Manor proved it to me again. The problems in our cities will not be solved overnight. But my experience as a lawman convinces me that reaching out is a start, that good people must stand together to defeat crime.

As my mother said, it means being on the right side of the law. *On God's side.*

Nancy Became Beautiful

BY WAULEA RENEGAR
CERRITOS, CALIFORNIA

*The story of a young woman who
found a friend.*

I first saw Nancy when she strode through the foyer doors of our church. Black mesh stockings stretched between white leather boots and a matching leather skirt. Her hair flamed crimson above blue eyes, and I was hypnotized as she moved toward me, for I knew Nancy to be, at twenty-two, a drug addict and a prostitute.

My protected, church-oriented life flashed neon for her. Even the dullness in her eyes could not veil the contempt she had for me. I suddenly felt I had wronged her, even though I had never seen her before. She walked past me without a word, down the aisle and directly into my husband's study.

Behind the closed door Nancy voiced her hatred for people like those straights in the foyer.

"Look, I'm a junkie. I'm a prostitute. I'm wanted by the police for hot checks. A pimp's out to get me for a bad debt." She opened her handbag and cradled a revolver in the palm of her hand. Her eyes were like flint as she spoke more to inform than to convince: "He'll never lay a hand on me." She shot a defiant look across the desk. "I'm in trouble. What are *you* going to do about it?"

For months my husband had been working with the local vice and narcotics squads and had seen women like Nancy.

23

The Holy Spirit let him hear her cry for help. "Is that all?" he asked calmly.

Her eyes narrowed. She apparently had expected shock, disgust. His calm acceptance threw her momentarily.

"Well?" she snapped.

"Well?" he countered.

She whirled around and stalked across the study to the outside exit. She paused, her hand on the knob. "I can't talk tonight; I'm high. Can I see you tomorrow?" Without looking around, she added, with effort, "Please."

"Two o'clock." He gave her our home address.

That evening my husband suggested that Nancy could be serious about wanting help. I nodded, casually accepting his advice to keep cool if she should call. Aware of my naiveté, he stressed that I should not show shock, contempt or rejection, regardless of her crude revelations. Those reactions would make her feel justified in returning to drugs with me as the culprit.

The next day Nancy was on my doorstep, her liquid eyes checking me sullenly. I invited her in; she scuffed past me, flopping into a chair.

"Wanting drugs is hard to get rid of," she began. Nancy was not one for small talk. She not only hit the nail, but she sent it crashing through the wood on impact. "When I want a fix, like now, the hardest thing to do is tell somebody. I know people want to help me. I know in my heart drugs are wrong. But when I need them, I don't want help—I want a fix." Her eyes rolled back in her head and I noticed how damp her face was becoming.

My eyes began to sting. I wanted to speak. I could not think of a thing to say. She opened her eyes and read me again. "Not this time," she said with genuine regret. She rose and left,

24

handing a paper to me as she passed. On it was written:

Dirty Sunday
I'll more than likely sit
completely still in my easy chair
with my two bare feet
And watch the reckless rats
rush off to worship and reek
in their role of the meek
Where there they will learn how to
make one more false face to wear
in their new money-making week.

That was Nancy. She walked up and asked for my hand, whacked it good, then became offended if I did not appreciate the slap. I was irritated, but kept in mind what my husband had said.

It has always fascinated me how people like Nancy eat the scum of life, experience the ultimate in rejection and humiliation, then hold on to the myth that they have a lease on honesty. Straight people, like myself, somehow could not know or be as honest as the degraded sufferer. Our motives and actions were suspect. Our words must be scrutinized for truth. Yet she expected me to accept every word she spoke as perceptive, knowledgeable gospel. She was batting me around like a ball.

I prayed much over my attitude. A change gradually came in my thinking. As her visits continued, I began to share with her what Christ meant to me. Sometimes she laughed. Other times I knew He was speaking His love to her. It was a startling revelation the first day I realized that Nancy was worth knowing even if she never changed. When Nancy realized I felt this way she no longer had the upper hand.

Then came the afternoon when she had been unusually

critical of people in general and she made a crack about "my sort of people."

"Look, friend," I snapped, "quit walking on my feelings. You don't like people cutting you down. I don't either. Being straight doesn't mean I don't have feelings. Friends don't walk *on* each other, they walk *with* each other." I extended my hand. "Friends?"

"You think of us as friends?" she asked in half-belief.

"You're drinking my coffee, aren't you?"

Something new began for Nancy. It had begun for me earlier. It was no more than a month later that she accepted Jesus Christ and ceremonially surrendered her needle with an announcement, "I'm kicking it, cold turkey."

I accepted the news in innocent, unabandoned joy. I was soon to learn the sentence she had passed upon herself. I listened to her labored breathing and heard her swallow air like a tiring swimmer. By degrees her voice deepened, slowed and drew out into nauseated groans. The groans extended, rising in pitch and weakening. I shall never forget her pain.

She began to attend church services three times weekly. "Boy, if my friends could see me," she hooted one evening after services. "Talking and shaking hands with all those *church* people." From habit, she made "church" come out sounding dirty. She flinched. "That's another habit I've got to break."

"That makes ninety," I parried without smiling. Her face exploded into a kaleidoscope of gaiety. She was beautiful.

From the first, the people of our congregation knew about Nancy. They accepted her conversion as payment in full to join the family. They had her in their homes for meals and they prayed for her as the mounting crises developed.

"I just don't get them. They know what I've been and yet they treat me like I'm one of them."

"Nancy, when will you quit enjoying self-pity?" I allowed my irritation to show. "Christ has done no greater favor for you than he has for them. He forgave us all, and not a one of us deserved it—you included. We can no more reject you than you can reject us. We're stuck with each other. You put up with us. We'll put up with you. And, thank God, Christ will put up with us all."

She looked stricken. I forced a smile and extended my hand. "Friends?"

Her blue eyes melted before me. Those were the first tears I had seen her shed. "Oh, yes," she choked, grasping my hand tightly. "Thank God, yes!"

Love Is Contagious
BY AMY WASHBURN

A lice was past retirement age for teachers, but it was her nature to fight against all rules, so it did not surprise us that she continued at her desk. She had always been outspoken and defiant.

The little clique of teachers of which I was a part ignored her most of the time. We tried to stay out of range of her stinging temper and sarcastic tongue.

It is understandable that we were quite upset when she was named principal of the school during midterm, replacing a woman who resigned because of illness.

The wrath of the new regime was felt immediately. Alice shouted commands and even berated us in front of our classes. She was harsh with the children too. Finally, we mutinied and went as a group to the superintendent.

He laughed off our charges saying, "No one can be that bad."

The following day, three of us were eating in the lunchroom when Alice—flushed with rage—marched to our table and accused us of talking about her. As she left, I suddenly felt sympathetic toward her. For the first time, I saw her as she really was—a pitiful, lonesome, old lady who needed our prayers instead of our censure.

I told the others and they agreed we should pray for her as well as ourselves, that we might gain a better understanding.

Slowly at first, we drew her into our circle. We remembered her birthday with little gifts. We invited her to eat with us. She who had been a stranger gradually blossomed into a warm human being.

We learned that her sister's husband had been ill, and it was Alice's paycheck that kept the family going. Her small niece had needed surgery for a heart condition, and Alice volunteered her savings for the operation. It became very clear why Alice's clothing was outdated and worn. Now we understood why she had worked past retirement age.

The miracle was the change that took place. Bit by bit, our love expressed in simple terms was reflected by her kindness. Love is contagious. Now our school is a better place.

I have heard the Sermon on the Mount many times, but it took Alice to teach me what Christ was talking about when He said, "Love your enemies, bless them that curse you, do good to them that hate you, and pray for them which despitefully use you. . ." (Matthew 5:44).

Even teachers need to go back to school some times.

Part Two

Friendship Lessons Learned Too Late

A Story of
Life and Death

BY JENNY WADE
NEW YORK, NEW YORK

*Seeing those horses in their pasture
gave Tim and me a sense of serenity.
We were going to need it.*

My friend Tim* died in 1986, at the age of forty-four. I'd known him for six years, ever since I went to work in Dallas, Texas, for a large corporation involved in communications technology. I liked him instantly, and liked him even more as I got to know him. His faith, his honesty, his devotion to his family—these qualities drew me to him. Tim's death changed the way I look at my life.

At the time I met Tim I was an ambitious twenty-eight-year-old woman who'd cracked the upper-management echelon in a highly competitive, traditionally male field. I worked hard. My career meant an awful lot to me. Because I was a woman, I always felt I had to work a little harder, a little longer to get the respect and success I wanted. Tim helped put things in perspective for me.

I remember once we were pushing hard on a project. Calvin, the vice-president of our division, let it be known that he expected us to work through the weekend if necessary. That didn't bother me. But one day during a project conference, Tim spoke up. "Cal, I know how important this thing is

*Name has been changed.

32

for the company, but I promised my daughter Terry I'd help her out with a bake sale Saturday at our church. I can't go back on my word. We'll have to find time during the week to get caught up."

Tim found time—coming in early, working through lunch—and the project was completed successfully on schedule. He always put in his share of overtime, though he never let it interfere with his family life. That's rare in the business world. So many executives' lives are consumed by the sometimes cutthroat realities of corporate life. Because of Tim I began to think of who I was outside the job and what I owed to others.

When Tim told me that he would be going into the hospital for gallbladder surgery, I was not too worried about him. After all, this was 1983. Medical science could repair just about anything that might go haywire in the human body, right? Besides, Tim had always seemed in such fine health.

"The doctors tell me it's a pretty routine operation," he assured me over lunch. "But I'll be off my feet for a while, and I won't be coming back to work full time for at least eight weeks. Or so they tell me," he added with a wink. I knew I'd see Tim back in no more than six weeks. I promised I'd pray for him.

While Tim was in the hospital I realized how much I'd come to depend on his attitudes to help straighten out mine. When I was having a problem, I'd usually take it to Tim. In the beginning we just talked about business, but gradually I trusted him enough to talk over more personal matters, such as my marriage or my faith. We both had strong beliefs. Sometimes we'd even pray together. In time I saw that a lot of people around the company felt they could turn to Tim.

And then there were the horses. Our company's head-quarters was located outside the city, and Tim's large office looked out on a pasture that usually had some horses grazing in it, beautiful horses. Often Tim and I would pause for a minute or two just to admire those elegant creatures. On hot days they would find a shady place to stand, tails switching. On cooler ones we'd watch them prance and play. On cold days the horses would gather close for warmth. Something about seeing the tranquility of those horses in their pasture gave us a sense of serenity, a glimpse of God at ease in nature.

I was eager for Tim's return, and a little surprised that it took him a full two months to recover. I remember being startled to see how his salt-and-pepper hair seemed to have turned mostly salt.

"How are you?" I bubbled that first day, popping my head into his office.

"Fine, Jenny. Great."

"Well it's great to have you back!"

But some of that old sparkle in Tim's eye seemed tarnished. *Oh well,* I mused, *surgery is always tough. He'll be okay.*

Gradually, inexplicably, Tim got worse. He lost weight. He barely had the energy to get to work in the morning. Some afternoons I'd peek into his office and Tim's eyes would be closed, his head hung in exhausted sleep. He seemed to age a decade in a matter of months.

Although Tim looked as if the world was beating on him, he didn't talk like it. If I needed advice or help, he was there. I felt a little guilty asking, though. Why should he expend any of his precious energy on my problems? But he did.

A year passed. An important project required Tim and me to fly overseas, the sort of trip that inflicts a nasty case of jet lag on even the hardiest traveler. The strain seemed nearly to kill Tim. He spent every spare minute collapsed on his bed in the hotel. When it came time to give another presentation, he'd pull himself together and perform brilliantly. But I was really getting worried. Then, not long after we got back to Dallas, Tim told me his doctors wanted him to spend two weeks at the Mayo Clinic in Rochester, Minnesota.

"They just don't know what's wrong," he sighed, his voice an exhausted whisper. "I don't have the stamina to have fun with my kids anymore, to help around the house—don't even get out of bed on weekends, don't feel like working, don't feel like anything. I feel like someone just took my life away."

This wasn't the Tim I knew. I could still glimpse a trace of his boyish good looks, but what I saw in his ravaged features was a terrible uncertainty, the kind of fear and vulnerability one sees in a very sick child who doesn't understand why he is suffering. That morning in Tim's office we prayed together, and the next day he left for Mayo.

I'm not sure what the doctors told Tim—I know they put him through a battery of tests—but when he got back he seemed reluctant to talk about it, and he continued to miss a lot of work, more than ever, in fact. I was traveling almost constantly. Between my hectic schedule and Tim's sick days, we barely got a chance to speak. I wanted to tell him about a job offer in New York that I thought I was going to accept. It was a big career move and I wanted his counsel. But every time I stopped by his office for a chat, all I would see was his neat desk and his empty chair.

Sometimes I would stand at the window gazing at the horses in the meadow. They seemed so content, yet I was so disturbed. I all but wondered out loud to God why innocent humans had to suffer, why Tim was sick. Over and over I'd ask Him to help my friend get better.

I accepted the job in New York, and when the day came for

me to leave, I went again to Tim's office, and again he was not there. I taped a note to the back of his chair where he was sure to see it. I was sure I'd see him again.

Not long after I had settled in my new job, I got a call from a friend at my old company in Dallas.

"Jenny," she said, "I have some very bad news. Tim has AIDS. He received contaminated blood during his operation. That's why he never got better."

On the outside I was silent, controlled. I didn't know what to say. But inside I was screaming, *No! No! No!*

"He came in Sunday when no one was here and cleaned out his office. He didn't say good-bye to anyone. People have tried calling him. He just won't talk."

I thanked her and hung up the phone. I wanted to throw it through a wall, but instead I replaced the receiver gingerly in its cradle. *It's just not fair,* I thought. I'd heard all about AIDS, a fatal illness caused by a virus that renders the human body defenseless against many diseases.

I decided I shouldn't call Tim. But what could I do for him? I couldn't force him to talk if he didn't want to. So I wrote him a letter instead. I knew that AIDS leaves the victim terribly debilitated. Maybe Tim was too weak to lift up his Bible and read. Along with my letter I included about fifty Bible verses that I'd copied on individual index cards, verses that had to do with hope and faith, suffering and healing, living and dying.

Months went by. I didn't hear from Tim. Not a call, not a note, not a word through a family member. I know now that Tim felt he couldn't face anyone, not even his friends, not even when he was dying. That's one of the most tragic things about AIDS: the stigma, the same irrational feelings that block out compassion, the same fear that in years past made "cancer" a dirty word. Tim must have felt ashamed, deeply ashamed, and afraid of the judgment that even his friends might pass on him.

Early in the winter of '86 Tim died in Dallas. The funeral was a strictly private family affair, and no mention of the cause of death was cited there or in Tim's obituary, which simply stated that he had died after a "long illness." What the obituary left out was that Tim had died alone and humiliated. I didn't think it was right that my friend, or anyone, should have to die like that.

I was in my office in New York when I heard the sad news. I stared out my window, thinking, *Oh, Tim, had you turned to us, we would have listened; we would have been there for you just as you were there for us. We wouldn't have blamed you for having the disease; we would have blamed the virus. Only God can judge. Maybe you forgot that.*

Outside my office window there was no peaceful pasture, there were no gentle, nuzzling horses. Instead there were only tall buildings with glass, and quicksilver elevators, and people like me, ambitious, shooting to the top just as fast as we could because we thought that was what was going to make the vital difference in our lives. I began to cry, not for Tim but for myself.

I felt an emptiness, a sense that my "getting ahead" was only for me, not for God. I'd been demanding to know from God why He had allowed such a horrible thing to happen to my friend. I hadn't received an answer. But sometimes we learn more that way. It wasn't necessary for me to know why God works in the world the way He does. I needed only to know what God wanted of me. Maybe there was nothing I could have done for Tim, but maybe there was something I could do about AIDS.

That day I called a list of organizations dedicated to helping people with AIDS and asked how I could help. I learned there was a lot of work that needed to be done by volunteers like me.

Now, two years later, I still work in my field, but only as a part-time consultant. I earn enough to take care of the essentials. I spend the rest of my time taking care of people with AIDS and talking to people who need to know more about AIDS. I give several presentations a week to corporations about AIDS in the workplace and about the nature of the disease in general. I speak to church groups who want to know how they can help. I explain that the disease is not casually, or easily transmitted, and that our biggest enemy in the fight against AIDS is fear and ignorance, and our greatest need is compassion. For the first time in a long time I feel as if I am doing something Tim's way—not just for myself but for other people and for God.

I still think abut Tim. I think a lot about the horses we used to watch in the meadow. I remember how they pranced on nice days, lazed in the shade on hot ones. But mostly I remember how on cold, hard days they came together for warmth. That's the way God intended it for us humans too, I think.

A Beautiful Friend

BY MARLENE THOMPSON
WEST LINN, OREGON

*Not even death could restrain
Helen's caring spirit.*

Helen was different. I'd always known that. Like me, she had Scandinavian roots and the blonde looks to prove it. Like mine, her husband was a high achiever, and like mine, her son was an only child. She and I loved people and a good laugh, and mutual friends came to the gatherings in our homes.

I watched my neighbor Helen. I'd watched her with others, outgoing and charming. I noticed her eagerness to sit and listen whenever someone needed a sympathetic ear. I paid attention to how Helen handled the inevitable crises of an adolescent son, a husband in a high-pressure job, aging parents, and illness. She'd shrug and smile and say, "Things will get better. I know."

Helen had hope. And I didn't.

Sometimes on summer weekends Helen and her husband would drive to our beach cottage on the Oregon coast, and my friend and I would slip away from the idle chatter and joking of the group to have a stroll and a serious talk.

My life had always seemed more tumultuous than the ocean's churning, and eventually Helen heard the bitter stories of my unsettled childhood. I confided to Helen some of the fears that plagued my adult life—fears about my being

39

abandoned once again. Fears that somehow I'd end up unwanted and alone.

Helen exuded strength. She looked delicate, but she had a
strength that seemed to come from within. When we were
together, she calmed my fears and made me feel strong.

In the late '70s, life for me seemed to splinter apart. My
father-in-law lost his life to cancer. My sister developed brain
cancer. My marriage of twenty years was crumbling.

Helen knew my anguish. During our phone conversations,
her comforting words boosted my crumbling spirits. And
she'd gently remind me: "Things will get better, Marlene. I
know they will. You'll see."

But I didn't see.

One March day in 1977 Helen dropped by. She was worried
about me. I'd been feeling depressed. We lived on the
Willamette River, and some days the thought of walking into
the river and sinking to the bottom seemed like the solution.
I wanted to die. I think Helen knew that.

"Marlene," she said, "you've been in my thoughts. I can only
stay a minute. I just wanted to leave this little gift with you."

Lovely Helen, always thinking of others. Always giving.

I smiled. "You've wrapped this so beautifully, Helen. You're
really too good to me. . . . Oh—" Now that it was unwrapped,
I hoped she hadn't noticed my disappointment.

Puzzled, I looked at the gift and tried to sound excited. "A
Bible! Just what I need to get myself through these horrible
days. How sweet, Helen. Thank you."

I held the small green Bible limply in my hand. Why would
I want a Bible? I knew as much about God as I cared to. Look
at the forty-one miserable years He'd given me. As soon as
Helen left, I tossed the Bible into a drawer.

A year later Helen died.

Things for me became worse. I had a stroke and was hospitalized. Just as I was recovering, my sister died of cancer; her two children, both troubled youngsters, moved into our home. Debts mounted. Then, on New Year's Eve 1980, my husband left.

I was in despair, and on a March day in 1981, a day when I longed to die, I began a desperate search for pills. My hands shook as I pulled out one drawer after another.

"Where did I put those pills?" I asked myself. "Where, where, *where?*"

And then my groping hand touched something that made me stop short. I brought it out. Helen's Bible. A note dropped from its pages and fell to the floor. I reached down, picked it up, and began to read. The note was addressed to me:

"Marlene, dear, read Psalm 34 and hang on to its promises. God can't lie! See you soon. Loads of love. Forever your friend, Helen."

Forever my friend. Not even death could restrain Helen's caring spirit. Somehow, here she was again, just when I needed her. Giving me comfort. Telling me I was loved. Pointing me to God.

I turned to Psalm 34. I read it once. "I will bless the Lord at all times . . ." And I read it again. ". . . I sought the Lord, and He heard me, and delivered me from all my fears." And again, ". . . and none of them that trust in Him shall be desolate." And each time I read that beautiful psalm of David I thought of my beautiful friend and her desire for me to find the Lord. It was a beginning, a nudge that sent me in search of Him.

I kept Helen's Bible on the kitchen table as a reminder and a help.

"See you soon," her note had said. And she'd kept that promise—on a day when I needed her most.

Next-Door Neighbors

BY MARION BOND WEST

*There was a chain link fence between
their backyards, but something more than
a fence seemed to separate these two.*

When I was offered the opportunity to take a trip back to Athens, Georgia, recently, I grabbed it immediately. More than anything else, I wanted to see the person I had never really known while I lived there, but who had since come to be an important influence on my life—my former neighbor, Grace Fields. I fully expected my visit to be filled with nostalgia, but I wasn't at all prepared for the discovery we made during our reunion.

Grace and I had lived next door to each other years ago, in the '60s. Our backyards in Athens were separated by a chain link fence my husband had erected to keep in our twin sons and the dog. But something more than that chain link fence seemed to separate Grace and me.

A busy young mother of four children, I was shy, often insecure and lonely. Grace seemed just the opposite. She and her husband, Dewitt, were older; they had never had children, and she appeared to have enormous amounts of time. I often noticed her from my kitchen window or as I hung out mounds of diapers; she was usually working in her picture-perfect yard.

Sometimes when I strolled the twins, I met her walking briskly around the block, long before it was fashionable to walk. We spoke politely. She seemed so orderly and mature that it was a while before I got up the courage to pay her a

43

neighborly visit. I took along two children in case I ran out of something to talk about.

We found her on her knees digging in her flower bed with a bright red trowel. I usually dug with a soup spoon when I had the energy to tend my neglected flowers. Her yard was breathtaking—small, but lush and manicured, enclosed by a quaint wooden fence with a marvelous squeaky gate. I felt like Alice in Wonderland entering another world. Grace wore a wide-brimmed straw hat and a pastel button-down-the-front flowered dress that she called "everyday." Somehow it looked spiffy to me. She was trim and wore well-worn sensible shoes and white socks.

Grace invited us inside for some lemonade. We followed meekly. She and my oldest child, Julie, talked intently and comfortably while I shifted Jeremy, one of the twins, from one hip to the other. She introduced us to her two overweight cats who lived inside.

I looked around and quietly marveled over a house that wasn't childproof, and I tightened my grip on Jeremy. My eyes lingered on a lovely silver bonbon dish that sat on an antique marble-top table. She had good books on her shelves and some paintings she'd done herself hanging on her immaculate walls. On the floor by the refrigerator were two china saucers from which her cats ate.

After that visit, we came back and forth to one another's homes, but we were careful not to allow ourselves to become vulnerable or close. She always phoned before coming over and assured me she'd stay only a few minutes. She always kept busy, and she seemed to enjoy being alone.

There began to be days when a depressive, deep loneliness and a fierce, unnamed longing seemed to pursue me like an enemy, usually late in the afternoon. Motherhood was more difficult than I'd imagined. I was tired and sometimes cried for no reason I could name. On those days I found myself standing at my kitchen window looking out at Grace's back door, which often was flung wide open so that the sun shone right into her kitchen. That sight never failed to soothe my emotions. An open door meant Grace was at home, and she was the most secure person I knew. I imagined her moving about, full of energy and joy in her quiet, lovely, and organized world.

All those years I lived behind Grace, I never dared to run to her open back door and admit, "Oh, it's so hard being a mother! I'm tired and I want to have time to paint and write. I've always wanted to write." I could not let her know, "I'm lonely and afraid some days," or ask, "Could we just sit in your kitchen and drink hot tea from your china cups and talk? Could we be . . . friends?"

Then before the twins started school we moved away—Jerry and I, our four children, and our black dog, Muff, which Grace never liked. Just as we were pulling away, I hopped out of the car and ran to my front porch and grabbed my flowering hanging basket and took it to Grace. I don't recall that we said anything significant.

Somehow we began to correspond—at first, little casual cards with careful, guarded messages, and then suddenly long, long letters in which we became less and less reserved. Grace returned some of my letters with the misspelled words circled in red (she had been a schoolteacher).

Soon I was pouring out my heart to her, writing details of my thoughts and dreams. She responded with picturesque letters faintly reminiscent of Emily Dickinson. I'd begun having articles, then books, published. Once she wrote, "One of the neighbors brought me your latest article. The whole neighborhood thinks it's quite good. However, I believe some of the

45

letters you've written to me are much better." Grace was one of the few people from whom I could take criticism.

Once, after years of letter writing, Grace added a P.S. to her letter: "Oh, how I miss you." Leaving dinner dishes and dirty laundry, I rushed right out to buy a card for her. It took nearly an hour to find the perfect one—a Persian cat resting in a Victorian setting.

I always answered Grace's letters the day I got them, ignoring whatever responsibility was most pressing. Her responses, always long in coming, were enormously anticipated and unbelievably delicious. How freely she poured her thoughts and feelings into those perfectly typed and spelled letters! I read and reread them.

When Jerry died just after he turned forty-seven, I heard from Grace—not a flowery sympathy card, but a neatly typed two-page letter in which she remembered Jerry with fondness and subtle humor.

After a few years I met and married a professor. And so it was that when he was asked to teach a short course back in Athens, I was able to go along one afternoon—to visit Grace. I was approaching fifty-three and expecting my fourth grandchild. Grace's own husband had died three years earlier.

Her house was just as I remembered it. Once again we sat on her living room sofa and talked. It was as though time had stood still. "Oh, Marion, I had this dress when you used to live here," she said with a laugh.

"Really? I thought it was new. It's back in style now and looks good on you."

After a while we went out to the backyard. She'd just had cataract surgery, so I offered her my hand. She took it, as though we'd always walked hand in hand. In her kitchen she paused to pick up her wonderful old straw hat; she never went outside without a hat to protect her face from the sun.

Grace's backyard was unchanged; woodsy, with violets and ferns, and squirrels and birds so tame they hardly noticed us.

Then we were at my old fence and we stood there holding on to it with both hands as though we were about to catch our breath taking a ride on a Ferris wheel. We did take a remarkable trip—to the past. It happened quickly and quietly, and we both realized it was happening.

The man who now owned the house had just cut the grass. It was late spring, and a wonderful fresh-cut-grass aroma filled the air. But for me in that instant it was as though Jerry had cut *our* grass. I was a young mother again, and my children would appear at any moment needing something. I must keep one ear tuned for a cry for help from one of the twins . . .

We stared long and hard across the fence. Finally Grace spoke. "Your dog always messed in the path I used when I came to see you. I always stepped in it."

I nodded, remembering. "Under the kitchen window my cat is buried."

"What was his name?"

"Little Kitty."

"Oh, yes. He was a good kitty. Yellow. I liked him."

We continued looking, remembering. Then we walked back toward her house, still holding hands. At her back door the late afternoon sun shone radiantly and formed a square of bright light that looked like a welcome mat on the floor. At long last I was basking in the warmth of Grace's kitchen.

Then we went to her sofa, and she began to tell me things I had not known. The words caught me by surprise.

"Marion, I was just your age now when you moved into the neighborhood," she said. "We'd just moved here too. I'd resigned from a position that meant a great deal to me to help care for my terminally ill mother. I nearly went crazy because I didn't have enough to do. I walked and walked the neighborhood to try to stay busy—and sane.

"You thought I was an old woman, I guess. You seemed to have everything. A young and healthy husband, four beautiful children, youth. I used to watch you from my yard; I knew you were too busy for me. And you had young friends. I was the old lady of the neighborhood. Did you know I cried when you brought me your hanging basket before you moved away? The flowers were half dead, but I revived them."

My heart pounded. All those years while we'd been neighbors, we'd allowed outward appearances and fear of rejection to form an invisible wall between us. We had thought we were too different to be friends. But in our letters those differences had faded.

The Bible says, "Man looketh on the outward appearance, but the Lord looketh on the heart" (1 Samuel 16:7). Finally we had come to see each other as God sees us.

After a long pause, Grace said at last, "Marion, thank you for . . . for coming to see me—and for being my friend."

To my astonishment, she cried openly. I threw my arms around her and we clung to each other for ever so long. I cried too. When we separated, we just sat, still holding hands, gazing out her picture window. Grace's enormous cat watched us, and the last reflected light of a lovely spring afternoon spilled through the window and surrounded us with a golden glow.

Brother, Can You Spare
A Pair of Socks?

BY FRED HOLMBERG
KENNEBUNK, MAINE

T he morning was cool and crisp. Mike and I sat on the stoop with light sweaters and a bit of chill, often rubbing our hands or standing up to get the circulation going. It was our fourth day in the Village.

The two of us had come to Greenwich Village, in New York City, as chaperones for a group of teenagers. Mike, a native New Yorker who had lived there most of his life, years ago, became accustomed to the moods of the city and the particular problems of the Village. Before leaving our country town in southern Maine he had warned me about the area. He had not warned me about myself.

Our teenagers were on their own for a while, discovering the quietness of the Village in daylight, an eerie contrast with the noisy bustling movements of people as they had jammed the sidewalks the night before.

A man approached us. He was obviously one of the local winos (a not too kind, yet common name applied to those who have drunk from the bottom of the bottle and beyond). The wino was covered with dirt, caked dirt which I thought must be accumulated from weeks, possibly months, of living out of trash barrels and bottles of cheap booze. His clothes were an assortment of castoffs—begged or stolen, torn and draped, lacking both buttons and zippers.

49

The wino came toward the two of us and looked up at where we sat on the stoop, five steps above the sidewalk. His eyes were glazed, yet strangely penetrating. He came up the steps to stare directly into my face. Had my eyes been closed I could have smelled his approach. The aroma of stale alcohol, dirt, and sweat were intermingled.

"Friend," said the wino, "I need a pair of socks. My feet are cold." His voice shivered as he spoke and he struggled to keep his balance.

I looked at him carefully and set in motion that analytical process that I have tried to train my mind to perform. The tabulation recorded the following:

It is true that he has no socks.

It is true that this man is cold.

It is true that he is having a chill, but it is probably from illness or the DT'S, and not from the cold.

It is obvious he is a wino.

Why does he want socks?

To wear? To sell for a bottle?

If I give him a pair of socks, it may contribute to his illness, and not help solve the problem of his chills. Besides, I have only one other pair of socks. They are clean, and I need them for the trip home tomorrow.

The computer-like analysis took a matter of seconds. Hardly a pause was noticed in the conversation. I said to the wino, "Friend, I don't have an extra pair of socks."

I turned, for the first time since the wino arrived, to see Mike's reaction. My mouth opened in disbelief. While I had so carefully analyzed the situation and made what I thought was a wise and scientific judgment, Mike was taking off his shoes. His hand now held the socks he had been wearing, and he reached his hand toward the wino. The socks were slightly dirty, but they looked warm and comfortable as Mike held them there.

"Here," he said, "take these."

The man looked different. He stood straight and for a moment his shivering ceased. His eyes brightened slightly and a warmth came through as he looked at Mike.

"Thanks, brother." His voice was stronger and the pleading tone was gone. "Brother, friend. It's not *your* socks that I need."

Mike tried to insist, but the wino shook his head and again smiled warmly at Mike. Then he looked at me. He drew his ragged clothes closely around him, as if to shut me out of his life. He raised his chin, tilted back his head and with all the staggering pride he could muster, walked off down the street.

Mike very slowly put his socks back on his feet. There was a silence between us. My mind wouldn't let the thought go. Some men respond to people like machines, while other men respond with the warm spontaneity of a man like Mike. Love and dignity come from men like Mike.

The Day I Became a Neighbor

BY MARION L. MCCLINTOCK
ANTIOCH, CALIFORNIA

Some years ago my husband, Earl, and our two young children moved to California from a large Eastern city.

I resented the move; it was a wrench to leave my family and friends. Worse, we'd put all our furniture in storage and had rented a small, furnished house in a nondescript neighborhood near Earl's new job.

The furniture was a motley array of unmatched pieces, nicked and scratched by former users, and would not respond to my vigorous cleaning and polishing.

But my greatest desolation was my utter loneliness. I would sit for hours and cry.

Earl suggested I make friends with the neighborhood women. But I was so homesick that I shrank within a wall around myself.

When Earl spoke of inviting people from his office for a visit, I said no. I was ashamed for anyone to see our home.

Another thing about the house that bothered me was the constant presence of flies and other bugs. I sprayed and swatted them all over the house. Whenever I went out or came in the house, I always stopped at the door and waved away any flying creatures that might be lurking nearby.

At the end of our street was a house with a porch where an elderly man sat for most of the day. I guessed that he was ill.

One day my doorbell rang. I hastily removed my apron and ran into the bedroom to smooth my hair and powder my nose. "It's probably just a door-to-door salesman," I told myself, but I was determined to present myself as a proper "lady of the house."

The forlorn-looking woman on my steps was not selling anything. Her hair was disarrayed, her clothes hung loosely on her, and her eyes were red and swollen from weeping. She looked familiar.

"Come in," I said. "Please sit down." While she was seating herself, I quickly whisked a small rug over the worn place in the carpet.

"I'm sorry to bother you," she said, twisting a damp ball of handkerchief in her lap. "I wouldn't have the nerve to ask you this, but I know you were always so friendly to my father."

I got up and turned off the radio so she couldn't see my startled look.

"Your father?" I managed to say.

"Oh, I'm sorry," she replied. "I guess you didn't know. He passed away last night." She fought back tears.

"My father," she went on, "was lonely in his last days. He did not know many people here. We came here from a midwestern town where we knew everyone and they knew us. You'll never know how much it meant to him to have you wave when you went in and out of your door. But he couldn't wave back. His arms were paralyzed."

Tears of shame rolled down my cheeks at the undeserved tribute. Then she asked if she could borrow a black coat she had seen me wearing. She wanted to wear it to her father's funeral. I eagerly got it for her.

When she left, I knew that I had reached a turning point. My self-pity and self-centeredness were the real causes of my loneliness. I had prayed for a way out of my loneliness and God had shown me the way. I knew now that I had to make the first move, the first overture to friendship.

That night I greeted Earl at the door with a smile and even overlooked the dirt the children tracked in behind him.

The next day I joined the other neighbors in providing homecooked meals for the bereaved family. A few days later, when I learned a young housewife on our block was expecting her first baby, I gave a shower for her at our home and invited all the other women on the block. No one seemed to notice the old furniture—nor did I anymore.

Months later we moved to another part of California. But this time there was no loneliness, no depressing period of adjustment. For I remembered the lesson I had learned from the old gentleman who mistook my angry arm waving for an act of friendliness.

This time it was no mistake—my greetings really were friendly. And I again found good neighbors by being one.

Part Three

Friends Pull Together and Learn from Each Other

The Quiet People

"Therefore when thou doest thine alms,
do not sound a trumpet before thee . . . ."
(Matthew 6:2)

A skinny kid dribbles a basketball on a crowded court, weaving through the other team. Cheerleaders shout and clap on the sidelines. The boy spots his coach and then throws the ball to a teammate, who shoots it into the basket. The cheerleaders explode, the crowd roars.

It looks like a regular basketball game, but there's something unusual about one of the Youngstown, Ohio, teams. Instead of stopping when the referee blows his whistle, the players stop after a signal from their coach. Instead of listening to the coach's voice, they read his lips or watch for hand directions. Instead of hearing the ball bounce behind them, they feel its vibrations on the floor. That's because all the kids on this team—and all their cheerleaders—are deaf.

George Naples is this unusual team's coach.

He's also the reason Youngstown has deaf basketball, volleyball, slow-pitch softball, and bowling teams. Until he retired two years ago, George was a watchman at the General Electric plant. Six feet six, he'd once played pro basketball for the Youngstown Cubs and had coached his church team. The inspiration for his new basketball project came from his youngest daughter, Elaine, who had been born deaf. Through her, George saw how sports might motivate deaf kids who tended to become apathetic and withdrawn.

When Elaine was ten, George went to her elementary

school, where there were special classes for the hearing impaired, and recruited boys for a basketball team. Some of them had hearing aids, some were profoundly deaf. Some read lips, others used only sign language. Most had never been on a team in their lives. But George soon had them dribbling and shooting the ball like any other player.

The next year, the team got a boost when a local fund drive enabled them to buy uniforms. "Their eyes just sparkled when they put them on," George says. Also that year, several girls joined as cheerleaders, including Elaine, doing organized yells coached by Elaine's sister. "It's important that they practice using their voices," says George, "especially in front of a crowd."

From the beginning, George's deaf players have always played against hearing teams ("anyone who will give us a game," he says). He thinks that's important. After all, he adds, "these kids are going to go out into the hearing world when they grow up."

Some of his athletes have gone on in sports. One boy played football at the University of Cincinnati, and another is an assistant basketball coach at a high school. Nobody can be more pleased by their success than George Naples, the man who showed them the way.

The Meaning of Hog Pen Gap

A tragic accident, an entire
community affected . . .

Loss

BY RICHARD H. SCHNEIDER
GUIDEPOSTS SENIOR STAFF EDITOR

On Saturday afternoon, June 20, 1987, the parking lot of
the first Baptist Church in Winter Haven, Florida, re-
sounded with the cries of happy voices. A group of twenty-
seven youths and their three counselors were boarding the
orange-and-white church bus. They were about to set out for
a "Life Week" camp at the Georgia Baptist Assembly in Toccoa,
north Georgia. The youngsters, ranging in age from twelve to
eighteen, had washed cars, held bake sales, and saved their
money for the trip, which would conclude with a tubing
excursion on the Toccoa River.

Amid a flurry of waves and chorused good-byes, the bus
pulled out of the lot. Everything seemed so right, so blessed.

Then why was Jeanne Pooser crying as she found herself
trotting after the bus until it disappeared around a corner?

"I don't know," she said later. "I just wanted to hug Cathy
one more time. I'm not an overprotective mother, but I cried
all that day."

When Monroe Tarvin helped his daughter, Carmen, onto
the bus, he hoped the heavy body-brace she wore for curvature

61

of the spine wouldn't be too difficult for her to maneuver. And sometimes, wearing it embarrassed her. As he walked back to his car, he picked up a nail lying by the bus's rear tire.

"Hmmm," he mused, "wonder what *this is about?" For some reason, it seemed to underscore the apprehension he had been feeling about the trip.*

But Gary and Gloria Jones had no such concerns. They were especially pleased because their fourteen-year-old daughter, Angela, was so happy. Three weeks before, in their company, Angela had accepted Jesus Christ as her Savior. The family had moved to Winter Haven from Ohio only eight months before, and the parents had been concerned about their daughter's making friends. But just the preceding day, Angel, as they called her, had remarked how much she loved living in Winter Haven because of all the church friends she had made.

As the bus lumbered down Central Avenue, some of the youngsters looked back at First Baptist with its cross-topped white steeple etched against the sky. The downtown church had served Winter Haven for a century, and its pastor, Rev. Ralph Harris, shepherded a flock of 2,400 members. For the most part, all was well at First Baptist. A decade earlier there had been a congregational split, and even in 1987 cool handshakes and averted eyes were not uncommon when congregants met former members who had started their own church.

On Monday morning the bus rolled into the Baptist camp-grounds in Toccoa, and for the next three days, the Winter Haven youngsters plunged into summer-camp activities, singing and swimming and playing games. In the evenings, they listened attentively to evangelist Dawson McAllister, who spoke of the suffering Jesus endured for their sake. Thursday evening, as they climbed into their bunks, all the talk was about Friday afternoon's inner-tube ride down the river in the Chattahoochee National Forest.

That night in Winter Haven, Gloria Jones was wakened by the voice of her daughter, Angela, calling to her. But Angel was 490 miles away in Georgia. Puzzled, she turned over and tried to go back to sleep.

The next day before the buses left the campgrounds for various destinations, their drivers huddled together in prayer, asking the Lord for safe journeys. Then First Baptist's driver and youth minister, Rev. Frank Brooks, counselors Jack Woods and Jerry Mixon and their young charges climbed into the 1974 International Lodestar bus for the three-hour drive to their river outing. Following in a van were six counselors, some of whom had children on the bus ahead.

The day was sunny and clear. As the bus wound through craggy Georgia mountains on the two-lane Richard B. Russell Scenic Highway, some of the youngsters hung over the green plastic seats chatting, and others read or listened to tapes of country group Alabama and gospel singer Al Holley. Someone suggested to Carmen Tarvin that she take off her back brace to be ready for tubing, but with no privacy for that, she shook her head. The vistas became breathtaking as the bus climbed toward the 3,500-foot-high Hog Pen Gap just south of Blairsville.

Occasionally the young passengers in the rear of the bus would wave at the van following behind. As Jerrie Harris lifted her hand to wave back in response, she found herself silently praying.

The bus reached Hog Pen Gap. It was just after 2:00 P.M.

Back in Winter Haven, Edith Blake, mother of Charles, thirteen, and Teri, who would turn fifteen that day, was in her kitchen preparing a salad for dinner guests that night.

Suddenly a wave of concern swept over her. *The children!* Not knowing why, Edith sank to her knees on the kitchen floor and began praying. Her husband, Don, stepped in and asked, "What are you doing?"

"Pray, Don, pray," she implored. "Something terrible is going on with those kids."

The church bus crested the hill. Ahead lay a three-mile descent, one steep enough to be avoided by most tractor-trailer drivers. Frank Brooks, however, had no qualms; he had handled this bus on steep roads before. But the heavy International began gaining momentum. There was a curve ahead. Frank lifted his foot and pressed the brake pedal.

Nothing happened. He pressed harder. The pedal went to the floor. Now the bus rumbled faster. Frank leaned into the steering wheel to make a curve. The tires screeched in protest.

In the van, David Buckley wondered if Frank shouldn't take it slower. But Frank was now powerless to stop the accelerating bus.

Laughter and chatter in the bus ceased. Foliage flashed by the windows in a green blur. With frightened eyes the youngsters watched Frank struggling to downshift. Counselor Woods, grabbing seat backs, worked his way up to Frank, and the two vainly fought the gear shift, then the emergency brake.

"Get down on the floor!" Frank shouted over his shoulder. Sweat beaded his forehead as he fought the wheel, asphalt curves speeding at him. If he could control it for another quarter mile they'd make the valley.

Screams filled the rocking bus as the youngsters lurched violently with each curve. Frank knew they would never make the next one. But if he could squeeze the bus against an oncoming cliff, perhaps he could slow it down. Gritting his teeth, he swerved into the side of the granite wall. With a metallic scream, the bus spewed a comet-trail of sparks, rocketed through seventy-five feet of ditch, ricocheted across the blacktop, slammed into the steel guard rail, flew into the air and rolled down the mountainside.

As the bus lifted into the air, David Earnest, fifteen, prayed amid flashes of flying luggage. *This is it,* he thought. *We're going home to the Lord.*

Greg Millman's head hit the luggage rack and everything went black. As Lana Metcalf prepared to die, she felt secure, knowing that everything she had been taught about the Lord was true.

The counselors in the van had lost sight of the bus in the curve. On rounding it, they saw no bus. An acrid stench of burning rubber filled the air, and skid marks pointed to a crumpled guard rail. In the shocked silence, Frank Metcalf said, "Let's all pray."

The counselors leapt out of the van, looked down the mountainside and gasped. Fifty feet below lay the crumpled bus. A few bloodied children were weakly struggling out of the twisted wreckage. Cries and moans of "I want my mama . . . I want my mama" sounded from within.

Cathy Pooser, thrown from the bus, lay silent and still, wedged between two trees. Paul Simpson, seriously injured, crawled to Cathy and, leaning over her, pleaded, "Breathe, Cathy, breathe!"

Leaving the van, David Buckley raced up the road to call for help while the other counselors scrambled down the mountain.

Sixteen-year-old Becky Durham, whose leg had been bayoneted by a metal rod, crawled up the embankment and collapsed. Two others joined her, Randy Mixon, thirteen, and counselor Sharon Buckley. Then Becky lifted herself and began to sing; Randy and Sharon joined her, their voices floating across the trees. "Amazing grace, how sweet the sound" . . . "Blessed assurance, Jesus is mine . . ." Soon the melody was drowned out by the wail of ambulance sirens and the rush of helicopter blades as rescue copters dropped from the sky.

Rescue workers, wary of causing a spark, edged through gasoline-soaked shards of metal and glass to extricate the injured. The Jaws of Life rescue tool had to be used in cutting victims out of the wreckage. Frank Brooks' face was shattered; Lance Metcalf hung moaning across a rail, his leg bent at a crazy angle; Kristy Kimbrell, trapped under a seat, was calm. Carmen Tarvin wasn't hurt badly at all; her rugged scoliosis brace had acted like armor, protecting her body from the crushing metal.

Then the rescuers, who had been encouraging the young-sters, suddenly became quiet. They had found a fourteen-year-old girl, dark curls framing her porcelain-like face. Angela Jones was already with the One she had so enthusiastically invited into her heart three weeks earlier.

One after another, ambulances and helicopters, heavy with wounded, roared off to six hospitals in the Atlanta area, where doctors and nurses waited in the emergency rooms.

Other people tried to retrieve remnants of the crushed suitcases and broken tape-players mixed with dirt-covered Uno cards, Frito-Lay corn chips and plastic cups. One man picked up a bloodstained, ragged brown Bible. Inscribed inside its front cover were notes one youth had taken at Life Week.

Gain

BY VELMA SEAWELL DANIELS
WINTER HAVEN, FLORIDA

Black clouds swept over the sun, sending an unseasonable chill through Winter Haven as I pulled up to the Publix Supermarket that Friday afternoon.

I planned to buy chocolate and nuts to make brownies for a church party to welcome home our youth group from their trip to Georgia. As church library director, I had worked closely with these young people since they were toddlers, and they were very dear to me.

As I parked in the lot, a friend ran up in tears. "Velma, it's terrible. Turn on your radio, quick!"

I flicked it on to hear a newsbreak: "A bus from the First Baptist Church of Winter Haven . . . careened down a steep mountainside in north Georgia. . . . Many are believed dead. . . . Details will follow."

Stunned, I shook my head in disbelief, then accelerated out of the lot down Central Avenue to the one place I felt closest to the youngsters. As I neared our church, a dark cloud lowered over it, obliterating the white steeple.

I chilled, but took strength in knowing that the love of Jesus was far stronger than any evil. Praying for the children, I rushed into the annex, already filled with distraught parents, reporters, and television crews. Broadcast technicians were setting up dish antennas in the parking lot. Someone spoke out: "Let's all take a moment to pray." Practically everyone, including newsmen, some wiping their eyes, knelt down on the hall floors.

Ten emergency phone lines installed by General Telephone

of Florida jangled constantly, and I joined the other volunteers handling them. A crowd had gathered around a computer in communication with the north Georgia hospitals. It printed out a staccato litany of injuries: broken neck, in coma, fractured jaw, punctured lung and broken arm, broken nose, lacerations, dislocated hip. . .

Cathy Pooser, with a broken neck and in a coma, was listed as the most seriously injured of all.

Weeping parents were consoled by Pastor Harris. Then he left for sad task of informing Gloria and Gary Jones about the loss of their daughter. Within two hours, the three of them were on a private plane fighting its way through a storm to Atlanta.

Incoming phone calls flooded our church's 294-PRAY number, and volunteers who normally offered solace to callers were now receiving assurances of help and concern. In spite of the thoughtful words, I could not help asking the old question: "Why?"

During the late-night hours when a lull stilled the phones, I overheard our minister of education, Bill Earnest, quietly comforting a parent. "Without God's loving-kindness, all of our children might have been killed," he said. "God protected them, and now He will mend their broken bodies, heal and restore them."

"God's loving-kindness?" I wanted to shout. "If He is pouring out His love to heal those kids, why did He let the bus roll off the road? If He is so kind, why did He let that little girl die?"

I slipped into the darkened sanctuary where cold rain peppered the stained-glass windows. The drops seemed to be saying, *Trust me. Trust me.*

But I had lost my trust. Through the lump swelling in my throat I prayed. When I finally simmered down, I began to feel His comfort inwardly.

68

Remember the lesson you taught these children through your library ministry?

I again saw the nine-year-old girls in their frilly dresses sitting before me as I told them: "We can trust God even when we cannot understand Him . . . and, most of all, when we simply cannot make sense of *why* things happen."

I settled back in my pew and prayed that good would come out of the tragedy. Then, taking a deep breath, I returned to the telephones where my husband, Dexter, was coordinating offers of help.

All through that night, we saw, in a very real way, the fulfillment of God's promise: "All things work together for good to them that love God" (Romans 8:28). For good did come from the disaster. And through it could be seen God's power and majesty.

In the midst of agony, tears, and helplessness, there was an outpouring of compassion, love, and caring. Two men sat in a corner of the annex deep in conversation, one comforting the other. The two had not spoken to each other in five years. There were others who had let little differences keep them apart, who were now in each other's arms, consoling. Before the night was over, a dozen private planes were volunteered to take anxious parents to the Atlanta hospitals. In Atlanta, strangers met each plane and arranged transportation to hospitals.

Much of all this was arranged by a man who I feel was sent by God. He was Charles F. Jenkins, special assistant to the president of Lockheed-Georgia Company, who seemed to be everywhere help was needed—in airports, at hospital bedsides, and eventually, in bringing the youngsters home. The Georgia governor's office phoned our church nearly every hour offering hope and encouragement. In the Georgia hospitals, local people stayed with the youngsters until their parents could arrive. One county sheriff, Rudy Roach, stayed with Kristy Kimbrell all night. "I've got a fifteen-year-old and an eleven-year-old of my own," he said. Many Georgians gave blood.

In Winter Haven, ministers and priests from other denominations, along with strangers from all walks of life, came to offer help. Restaurant owners, not members of the church, worked their way through the crowds, balancing trays of sandwiches, coffee, and doughnuts.

Today the good continues. One can feel it everywhere in Winter Haven, not only in our church but on the streets and among the business people. There are no more church factions; more and more neighbors are taking time to chat, store personnel being more helpful.

Little by little, as the days went by, the youngsters came back from the Atlanta hospitals. All except Cathy Pooser. She still lay in a coma.

But at last, on a hot August afternoon, Dexter and I stood in a crowd gathered at the Orlando airport to await the plane bringing Cathy Pooser home.

All of the other survivors who were able had joined in the welcome; youngsters with stitches across their faces, gaps where teeth used to be, legs in casts. A news reporter asked a young blonde girl with a broken jaw, "How can you face what happened to you?"

Monica Thomas tried to smile through her clamped teeth. "I still have nightmares of the bus rolling down that mountain and I scream," she said. "But when I quit thinking of my own aches and pains and think about the others, I seem to get through it all the better."

"There's the plane," cried someone. The plane landed, and

a cheer rose as Cathy Pooser was carried down the steps in a stretcher. She was not fully conscious, but her eyes were open. A hush fell over the crowd as all joined hands in a prayer of praise and thanksgiving for her homecoming and for the recovery that her doctor predicted would eventually be complete.

As the crowd began to disperse, I saw a young newswoman turn to a young man on crutches. He was one of the passengers injured most severely. "Are the parents who lost their daughter in the accident here today?" she asked.

I shall never forget that young man's answer: "No, ma'am, they're not here," he said. "The folks who lost their daughter, Angie, are real good friends of mine. And when I asked them how they could stand losing her, they told me something I'll always remember.

"'You haven't *lost* someone,' her parents said, 'when you know where to find her. And we know where to find Angie—in heaven.'

"And you know, ma'am," he added, "this is how we are all getting through this—knowing we will definitely be with Angie again."

My Good and Faithful Friends

BY MARY GLADYS BAKER
WAURIKA, OKLAHOMA

*I shivered as much from fear as
from the cold. How long before
someone would find me?*

"Hi, Mom!" My daughter, Dale, greeted me when I finally limped my way to the ringing telephone. "I just wanted to remind you that the basketball games starts at six-thirty."

I might be old and forgetful, but there wasn't much chance I'd forget that the University of Oklahoma was playing Louisiana State on television that night last January. Lord knows, when you're eighty-four years old and have outlived your husband and half your friends, you find your pleasure where you can. And I found basketball, particularly Oklahoma basketball, a real source of pleasure.

"Thanks for calling," I said to Dale as I glanced at the ice on the kitchen window and at the snow-shrouded dusk beyond. "I'm warm as July and ready for the tip-off."

Now, I knew that Dale hadn't really called to remind me about the game. She'd called to check on me. Not that I minded. I'd had eleven surgeries and enough strokes to leave my left leg dragging. Sometimes I felt the same as that left leg, dragging and worthless.

I went to the back door. Little Bit, my ten-month-old

73

Labrador retriever, followed me as I looked for a glimpse of Scout, her seven-year-old counterpart who ruled the back-yard and hated to be inside. Scout's bed was protected from the snow on a covered patio, but with the setting of the sun the temperature dropped fast. I figured now was as good a time as any to replace Scout's damp quilt with the dry one I had stored above his bed. I'd give him his bedtime cookie too. Both my dogs loved cookies, particularly vanilla creams.

I put on a pair of old tennis shoes without laces. "Stay inside!" I ordered Little Bit as I stepped out the door. The bitter wind whipped through my nightgown as I hurried across the patio toward Scout's wagging tail. And there, suddenly, I slipped.

The hard concrete of the patio jarred the breath out of me. I opened my eyes with a moan and tried to sit up, but I couldn't move my legs. I ran a shaking hand across my left hip, where a hard knot jutted out at an awkward angle. I'd broken my hip! *Stay calm. Think.*

Scout wandered over and sniffed me. His cold nose assured me that this wasn't a nightmare. Shivering, I looked around for help, but my eyes weren't focusing right. I reached up and touched my face and realized my glasses were gone. Squinting, I saw them across the patio, where the force of my fall had thrown them.

The only sound I heard was the wind crackling in the frozen trees. Eerie light from the television flickered through the window, casting marauding images on the snow. I shivered as much from fear as from the cold. How long before someone would find me? Dale had already called this evening. Everyone was buttoned up at home thinking I was watching the game. No one would check on me until tomorrow. *God, help me! I can't survive out here all night.*

"Help! Help! Somebody help me!" I screamed, even though nobody could hear. Scout raised his ears with curiosity, then huddled back and curled into a ball on his bed. I looked at the back door—fifteen feet and one glass storm door was all that separated me from warmth. With a determined effort I struggled again to sit up. No use. I raised up on my elbow and looked around. Scout's chain! It was thirty feet long and connected to a patio post. I pushed myself onto my side and reached for the chain. I had it!

Holding the chain with both hands, I closed my eyes and pulled, dragging myself along inch by inch. Pausing to catch my breath, I opened my eyes to check my progress only to find that the chain was pulling me *away* from the door! I choked back my frustration, propped myself on one elbow and began dragging myself in the right direction. There were three steps leading up to the door with a low railing beside them. If I could reach that railing, maybe I could pull myself up the steps.

I felt sand grinding into my elbow as I moved. My tennis shoes fell off, causing my heels and ankles to scrape against the concrete. "Thank You, Lord, that there's no ice on the patio," I whispered.

The effort of pulling myself warmed me a bit as I inched toward the door. I almost shouted when I reached the railing beside the steps. I reached up and pulled, then pulled again, but pull as I might, I couldn't lift myself up the stairs. I'd gone as far as I could.

Loneliness covered me like a cloak. All those years of frantic bustling raising young'uns had faded into long hours of passing time. How much time did I have left? It was hard, sometimes, to be beholden to people, but I'd never experienced total helplessness before.

"God, I've done all I can do. Please don't let me freeze to

death," I prayed through chattering teeth.

Little Bit, whimpering, watched me through the storm door. I was close enough to see her now, even without my glasses. Barking, she hurled herself against the door. Again and again she threw herself against the glass until, finally, the door flew open. She bounded down the steps and crouched beside me, laying her cheek against mine. Warm breath panted against my frozen face.

"Good girl, Little Bit," I crooned, trying hard to swallow the lump in my throat. Little Bit licked my cheek, then, as if assured that I was alive, ran off to play with my glasses. Scout wandered over and curled up behind my back. I could feel his heart thumping against my spine; the rhythm of his breathing was hypnotic. Soon the sighs of his sleep mixed with the sound of the wind.

Sleep. I'd always heard that freezing people should never go to sleep. They might not wake up. My face felt blistered by the cold, my elbows screamed with pain, but worse, I couldn't feel the cold on my feet.

I tried to imagine the hottest day I could remember. Those days before air conditioning, sweltering in the Oklahoma sun. Only I couldn't. I couldn't remember anything except the cold that chilled my very core. How long had I been there? I looked at the familiar sky and guessed it was after midnight.

The wind picked up, its gusts slapping me with icy fingers that lifted my gown, shooting pain down my leg. I gasped for breath as the wind whipped across the snow, stinging my face with ice crystals.

Jesus! The cry came from deep inside me. "Jesus." Just whispering the name made me feel stronger. How long had I been trusting that name? Was it fifty years or sixty years now? Years of reading the Bible and attending the Church of Christ . . .

So, was this what it had come down to? Me meeting my Maker by freezing to death? I thought of my oldest daughter fighting her deadly battle against cancer. None of it made any sense. Her having cancer while an old woman like me just kept hanging on. Yet something deep inside me clung to life.

Suddenly I remembered the Scripture Paul wrote while he was in prison waiting to die: ". . . I also suffer these things: nevertheless I am not ashamed: for I know Him whom I have believed . . ." (2 Timothy 1:12). The words took on new meaning as I repeated them aloud.

"Father God," I prayed, "I'm suffering out here in this cold, and I don't believe You'll let me freeze to death. I'm trusting You to save me, but whether I live or die, I believe in Jesus."

A few minutes later Scout stirred, then stood and began walking away, removing my only shield from the north wind. The wind blasted my back, and my body began jerking so hard I could barely talk. "Scout, come back, boy. Come back and lie down." He paused and looked back at me, then trotted toward his bed.

I watched in amazed silence as Scout sank his teeth into the corner of the quilt on his bed, backed up and began pulling the blanket across the patio. Little Bit pranced around while Scout tugged the quilt over my body.

"Good boy, Scout!" I sobbed, pulling the damp quilt up around my shoulders and tucking it under my elbow. The quilt, tattered and potted with holes, blocked the buffeting wind. Scout lay down and stretched his long body beside my back, radiating warmth like warm coals.

I raised my head to check on Little Bit. If only I had my glasses. *Ask her.* The thought came unbidden.

"Little Bit, could you bring my glasses?" Little Bit trotted across the patio, picked up my glasses and brought them to me. *Thank you, Jesus.*

My broken hip was numb, but my leg felt like raw nerves exposed to the cold. What I wouldn't give for a hot water bottle or a heating pad. *Ask Little Bit.*

What a strange thought. *Little Bit can't go inside and get my heating pad. . . . Of course, she probably feels as warm as Scout . . . and she did get my glasses. . . .*

"Little Bit, come here, girl. Look at my legs. Could you lie down right here on my left leg?" Her liquid eyes met and held mine for a moment before she lay gently where I had asked her. Warmth from her body radiated through the damp blanket, creating moist heat that seeped into the bone, easing my pain. I felt cradled between the dogs, their satiny black coats a vivid contrast to the moonlit snow. Blood began pulsating through my frozen limbs as if answering the rhythm of their heartbeats.

"Little Bit, you and Scout are going to get as many cookies as you want when I get back on my feet."

I watched clouds drifting in the night sky while I talked to God, Scout and Little Bit. The first rays of sunrise cast a crimson flush over the snow, bringing several degrees of instant warmth. The sun was high in the morning sky when I heard a car stop by my mailbox.

"Help!" I croaked, my hoarse voice barely above a whisper. I heard the door open and knew Dale had gone into the house. "Oh, Lord, You've brought me through the night. Please don't let Dale leave without finding me."

"Mother!" Dale screamed when she saw me. Soon I was loaded into an ambulance that headed to Wichita Falls, Texas, as if its tail were on fire. I had surgery to repair my broken hip but refused surgery to amputate my frostbitten heels. During the fifteen days in the hospital, as my damaged heel peeled off in layers and fresh new baby skin took its place, it seemed as if my whole life had been peeled away and made fresh.

When I came home again, I thought back to the story of Balaam in the Old Testament and how God used a donkey to save him from the angel of death. I smiled as I handed Scout and Little Bit yet another vanilla cream. If God could use dogs and donkeys, I guess He still has use for an old gal like me.

Grandma's House

BY RUTH DOWDELL
OKLAHOMA CITY, OKLAHOMA

The Oklahoma City bus I rode home after a day of looking for work turned onto Northeast Twenty-third Street only blocks from where I lived. We passed a house, now boarded up.

"Place was condemned because of the plumbing," said the man sitting next to me. "Whole family out on the street."

Leaning my head against the window, I thought of my own nightmare. Where would *we* be if the authorities found out about *my* ramshackle house? The sewer line had collapsed. The gas had been shut off, leaving us without hot water. And the wiring would smolder if too many lights were turned on at once. I'd guarded our situation from most folks, but crumbling bricks and a tattered roof told the story. The house was sagging on its very foundation.

And now I had an even bigger worry. I had agreed to host a Bible study—in *my* house. And I was beginning to panic.

At my church, Faith Tabernacle, small groups of men and women met in homes around the city for Bible study. One Sunday in church I'd been thinking of joining a group when I heard an inner voice say, *You host a Bible study, Ruth.* Somehow, in the comforting confines of that massive brick sanctuary, feeling the presence of God, I believed it was the right thing to do, and I signed up as a hostess. Now it seemed like pure folly.

The bus groaned to a stop, and I climbed down and started the walk to my place, wondering, as I did every day, how I could

81

go on. What chance did a sixty-three-year-old, out-of-work widow with a fourth-grade education have trying to keep up that house and support an unemployed daughter and six grandchildren on $500 a month? "Lord, only You can help me," I kept saying.

When I rounded the corner, I let out a slow breath of relief. There was no "Condemned" sign.

As the date of the first Bible study approached, I was almost relieved when my grandchildren came down with chicken pox. On the night of our first meeting, the group had to gather at another home.

When I arrived for the Bible study that evening, I sank into plush carpet as I walked across the living room of the host's home. *Oh, Lord,* I prayed, *let them choose this as the regular meeting place.*

After several meetings the leader said, "Ruth, how about two weeks from tonight at your place? Your grandchildren should be over the chicken pox by then."

I watched golden light flicker on highly polished furniture. *I just can't let these people see my house,* I thought.

"Ruth?"

"Yes . . . that'll be just fine," I answered, forcing a smile.

Days dragged by while I wrestled the problem. How could God ask me to do this? I stood in the living room looking at the sofa that had been my mother's, and the mismatched chair that I'd moved over the spot where rain had warped the floor. There was no way to make it better. "Lord, you've *got* to help me," I said.

Instead, it got worse. One day, after a heavy rain, the ceiling of my bedroom collapsed.

I can't do it, I thought. *I can't sit in a house with holes in the ceiling and host a Bible study on excellence in the Christian life.*

Even as I made my decision, guilt began to nibble at me. I sagged onto a kitchen chair. God wanted me to host the Bible study. I knew I couldn't cancel, no matter how bad the house was.

The night of the meeting I paced the floor, forcing a smile when the first car stopped outside. But when I swung the door open, the car was pulling away. Minutes later it returned and a woman stepped out. "Ruth?" she called.

"Yes, come on in!"

"Oh, I didn't think anyone lived here. . . ."

Help me, Lord. I'm giving you what's left of my pride. I plastered a smile on my face as a dozen people arrived, and pulled extra chairs from the kitchen while they stood politely, looking around. Was that nervous laughter I kept hearing? Then the room became quiet except for the rustle of pages as Bibles were opened. I tried to concentrate on the Scripture, but I found myself glancing around. *What could they be thinking?*

Finally, unable to stand the strain, I said, "Look, this might not be the best place to meet but we came here to talk about the Lord. I know it looks bad, but let me tell you, I believe that God is at work in all this, and He's got something better for me, maybe just around the corner."

"You're right, Ruth," one man said. "The important thing is that we're here to learn." Murmurs of affirmation filled the air as we settled down to study the Scripture.

A few weeks later a woman from the Bible study group stopped by for a visit. I'd just settled my guest at the kitchen table and reached for a teacup when a sudden *swoosh* and *thud* echoed from the living room. I looked up and froze. The living room ceiling had caved in, littering the floor and sofa with rain-soaked moldy Sheetrock.

A flash of humiliation struck me. My guest had witnessed

this scene! The next instant a new thought occurred: *It could have fallen on the Bible study group!*

"Ruth!" I heard, as though from a distance. "Ruth, what are you going to do?"

"First," I said, almost giddy with relief when I thought of what might have happened, "I'm gonna get the trash can and a broom."

"But, Ruth, what are you going to *do?*"

For the first time I saw the agony on my friend's face. "Look," I said, putting my arm around her, "God's just getting this ceiling out of the way so He can put up a new one!"

The furniture was dry by the time the Bible study group met at my house again. I used plastic garbage bags to line the rafters.

I felt some of the old uneasiness when folks began to arrive. But then someone asked, "Did you get a new decorator, Ruth?" and I laughed so hard I gasped. The tension was broken. I explained the garbage-bag ceiling, and we settled down to study. Still, I couldn't help wondering, *Will they come back?*

They *did* come back. The plastic bags were replaced from time to time, and new chunks of ceiling fell, but the Bible study continued to meet.

Fabian, my daughter, finally found work as a chef at a health food store, which eased our financial situation. The months went by, but despite my constant pleas, God seemed deaf to my request for help in fixing up the house.

Then one day my elderly aunt and uncle in Detroit wrote asking me to come stay with them. They were getting on up in years and needed my help.

"Go ahead," Fabian urged. "I can get some friends to watch the kids."

I used my $150 Social Security check to buy a round-trip

super-saver ticket to Detroit. I was gone for two months, but during all that time I was thinking of home. Were the kids all right? Would they turn on too many lights? Would the house still be livable when I got back?

Finally I came back to Oklahoma City. There in front of my house, I saw a crowd gathered. *Something bad has happened,* I thought. People filled my yard; cars jammed the road.

And then I saw it; across the front door was a sign. A chill rippled up my spine. I knew what it must say: *Condemned!*

Pressed by the crowd, I moved closer, trembling. I looked up in confusion and read the sign: WELCOME HOME, GRANDMA!

What on earth . . .?

I glanced around as people began to cheer. I saw Caroline Callahan, a mission-team leader from my church, and members of my Bible study group, my family, neighbors . . .

Then I caught a glimpse of the roof—a new roof! My gaze swept the front of the house. There was new paint. The windows were repaired, sitting snugly in their frames.

"Is this my house?" I screamed.

"Come inside and see!" Caroline insisted. Inside, there were no plastic bags in the rafters. The walls and ceiling had been replaced. Everything was freshly painted. The floor was shining and smooth—no warps, wrinkles or water stains. I looked at Caroline. "Has the floor been replaced?"

"Yes," she nodded, with a grin, "but first the foundation was repaired."

My house had been rebuilt from its foundation!

I started running from room to room, screaming as I opened each door. The kitchen had been enlarged. There were new cabinets, a stove, refrigerator—a *dishwasher!* I gasped at the sight of central heating and air-conditioning. And there was a shiny black electrical box—the whole house had been rewired.

"Oh, man, this is neat!" I cried.

"Plumbing was fixed too," Caroline said, urging me on. I flung open the bathroom door and shouted at the sight of a new shower.

My church usually does this type of rehabilitation project in Mexico, but at the urging of my Bible study group and Sunday school class, they decided to restore *my* house instead. The Community Action Program provided the roofing materials, and Oklahoma Gas and Electric contributed the insulation. Otherwise, all money, materials and labor were donated by church members, including close to 4,000 hours of volunteer labor.

God had answered my prayers after all, but in a way I would never have imagined. Instead of helping me get the house fixed so I could host the Bible study, He had me invite the group over so *they* could rally around me and see to it that the house was repaired. Now I have a new house, a great group of friends—and a whole new insight into the unexpected ways God works.

Isn't God *something?*

Lori and Me

BY TERESA SCHANTZ
MOBERLY SENIOR HIGH SCHOOL
MOBERLY, MISSOURI

My mind was still caught up in vacation excitement as I walked off the plane into the Kansas City airport, exchanged hugs with my parents, and tried to answer all the questions they threw out at me. I'd been away visiting my cousins for a few weeks.

"Gosh, it's going to be great to see Lori," I interjected, referring to my best friend. Two loners, Lori Dailey and I met in the seventh grade. We fast discovered that together we could attack life and its problems, and win. A rare friendship developed in which neither of us was the "leader" but instead we shared decisions and talents. I think our love for each other was an echo of a verse from 1 Samuel 18:1: "And it came to pass . . . that the soul of Jonathan was knit with the soul of David, and Jonathan loved him as his own soul."

Mom spoke softly. "I think Lori really misses you, too. You see, she's had kind of a shock. There was a fire. Lori's home is partly destroyed."

Now I was scared for Lori. For indeed, the fire had all but ruined the Daileys' home. Its first flickers had rapidly enveloped the kitchen. Later, as I walked through the ruins, I found nothing of the colorful, woodsy room so familiar to me. The kitchen now resembled a tomb with its black, charred walls; only ashes remained where appliances and furniture had stood. The phone on the wall had melted, and the plastic had oozed down, desperately clinging to the wall. Lori's room had the air of having been caught by surprise. Clothes still lay where she had tossed them on the bed; it was spooky.

It was many months before the Daileys found a new home and slowly replaced the necessities. Their church and friends helped with many prayers and various donations.

Although it had been a terrible experience, to my surprise it wasn't Lori who was hurt by the tragedy—but me! A gnawing feeling took over the pit of my stomach. Though I had been a lifelong Christian, Lori had only become a Christian during our freshman year in high school. Now, because of the fire, Lori had a new-found strength that I felt lacking in myself. People's incessant interest in Lori and her needs began to irritate me. I found myself standing, puzzled, before a wall of jealousy. Could I actually be jealous of Lori's fire?

Talking to Lori one afternoon, I found that the fire had actually increased her peace of mind and rearranged her priorities.

"When something like a fire happens," she said, "you find out that *things* really don't matter that much to you."

Looking around my own spacious room bursting with *things*—records, music, a desk my father had made me, pictures, sentimental mementos and awards—I felt like a bumbling hippo wallowing in selfishness. To have these objects destroyed would really hurt me, I knew. They seemed like an important part of me.

I think it was that day that I realized what was wrong with me. Lori's young faith had been tested, and she had come through the winner. The faith I'd felt secure in had never really been tested. Now, I found myself almost wishing that something terrible would happen so that I could experience what Lori had.

My life seemed so ordinary. My father and both grandfathers being Christians, my faith had come naturally to me. Our family had experienced no gruesome deaths or horrifying accidents. My life had been woven with the various experiences of a preacher's home—both good and bad—and they had made me strong. Or, at least, I had thought so. But my life had lacked the dramatic incident that would set me apart from the crowds of average Christians.

Everything about my life had been too simple, too perfect—frighteningly so. Luke 12:48 now became almost a threat: "To whom much is given, of him will much be required." Was the Lord going to be terribly severe with me because He had given me so much, had allowed me to be so protected from tragedy?

Then one day my dad made a statement in a sermon that helped me. He said, "The great people are those who believe that nothing is ordinary. Every person, every job, every time, and every place is very special. And because they really believe this, life for them, in fact, becomes extraordinary."

It made me ask myself, "What's wrong with being ordinary?" Must I do great evil in order to come back and find God? Was my faith puny because I was reared in a Christian home with a few of the labor pains of growing up in a sinful world? Was I inferior spiritually because I had no dramatic story of faith to tell? Should I be ashamed of good health and a happy home?

So, strangely, Lori's fire brought spiritual victory not just to her, but to me. For the first time I really appreciated being just an ordinary person with no exciting experience to tell. Being an average person is a great blessing. For the ordinary person can, by God's power, be the most powerful force of all—a simple life used faithfully for His glory.

Part Four

Love to the Rescue

Evidence of Things Unseen

BY WAYNE AND SAM DRASH, GALLATIN, TENNESSEE
AND THOMAS MUNGEN, MEMPHIS TENNESSEE

Wayne Drash: *Student*

In November 1981, when Jennifer Adams* disappeared, I was in fifth grade. Jennifer's picture was all over the TV news and the papers. She was fifteen and pretty, with black hair and friendly eyes. The Adamses lived in a nice part of town, and Jennifer went to a high school five blocks from our elementary school at Christ United Methodist Church. The police thought she'd run away, but no one who knew her believed it. She just wasn't like that. Why would she take only jeans and her cheerleading outfit? All of us kids were fascinated and scared at the same time. Stuff like this didn't happen in our town. We all thought we were safe—at least at home. Now we weren't so sure.

Phone calls started coming in. One person said he had Jennifer, and he gave a list of demands: money, a car, merchandise from the store Jennifer's uncle owned. The police tracked the caller. It was a teenage boy. The whole thing was a hoax.

By early December, in desperation, the family offered a reward for any information about her. Dozens of calls and letters poured in to the police station. They followed up on anything that seemed promising. Nothing led anywhere. A month after her disappearance the police didn't hold out

*Name has been changed to protect victim's privacy.

much hope. Christmas and New Year's passed, then Valentine's Day as well. With March came spring. By then a lot of us weren't thinking so much about Jennifer anymore. Not so my dad.

Sam Drash: *Wayne's father*

In 1982 I was headmaster of Christ Methodist Day School, where my son Wayne was a student. I usually arrived at school an hour before the students. On the morning of March 4 I'd just come in when I noticed something unusual on my desk—a paper towel with pencil writing on it:

"Please help me. My name is Jennifer Adams. Call my father George Adams and police. My phone number is 555-1818. I am in the attic with kidnapper. Please, I want to go home. Call police. We come down at night and walk around in the dark. God bless you, Jennifer Adams."

I stared at the note for maybe two minutes before calling my secretary into the office. She told me the fourth-grade teacher had found a note similar to this one the week before. I remembered the earlier hoaxes about Jennifer. But this one was different. No one had had time to put this note in my office—except Wayne, who had ridden to school with me, and my secretary. I trust Wayne completely, but to be certain, I asked him to come into my office and write his name and our address. His handwriting clearly didn't match the writing in the note. I called the police.

They arrived quickly. The chief investigator assigned to Jennifer's case studied the note, then asked to speak to me privately.

"Mr. Drash, you did the right thing by calling us. But 'Jennifer notes' have become a kind of local pastime, and a school can be full of mischievous kids. Of course, we'll check

94

it out anyway. The note refers to an attic. . . ."

"The church has three houses on our property. Each one has an attic," I said. Together we went to the houses and climbed to the attics. The police went room to room as well, and then searched the church building itself. Nothing.

As they prepared to leave, the detective said quietly, "That note spoke of a kidnapping, but we'd have heard from the perpetrator by now. It's been four months. I'm sorry, Mr. Drash. Jennifer Adams is probably dead."

His words hit me hard. If this note was a sick joke by one of our students, I wanted to know who it was. That morning I devised a spelling test using the distinctive letters in the note, and asked each of the teachers to give it as a pop quiz. None of the kids' handwriting matched.

For the rest of the day, I couldn't concentrate on my work. The note was just another of the strange things that had been happening. Last October I'd brought in a hand drill to put up some shelves in the office. When my wife, Ginny, asked me to bring it home the next week, it was gone. I'm not the type of person who usually misplaces things . . . but I'd lost a stopwatch as well, and a camera. My office is watched during the day and locked at night. How could anyone have gotten in?

Then there were the pecans. Each Christmas the local Lions club sells bags of pecans as a fund-raiser, and I brought a whole box to sell at the office. Soon afterward bags began disappearing from the box.

One Thursday night I determined to catch the thief. After the school staff left, I locked my office door and turned out the lights. As night fell I crawled to the floor to hide under my desk. When I finally left at 11:30 my back was killing me. The next morning six bags of nuts were missing.

Teenage pranksters made sense, of course. But somehow I

believed the note was real. Why did I seem to be the only one who believed it?

On Sunday, March 14, my wife and I and our three boys went to the early church service and sat in the front pew. Our middle son, Mike, picked up the pew Bible next to him. There was a paper stuffed in it. We all watched, transfixed, as he pulled out a paper towel. It was another note from Jennifer Adams, dated that very morning.

Suddenly I knew this was no prank. She'd been in this very spot only a few hours before. But how could that be? *Where could she be?*

I studied the note. This time it said "*church* attic." As soon as the service ended, I hurried to the stairs at the back of the sanctuary. The balcony at Christ Methodist comes down at a slant, forming a triangular room underneath. *She has got to be hidden in there,* I thought.

I spent about ten minutes searching as much of the room as I could get to. Part of the room was cluttered with stacks of insulation and pieces of plywood piled atop some two-by-six-inch wooden supports. I was unable to find any evidence that anyone had been in that room. I left feeling very puzzled.

That evening I replayed everything in my mind. *What's going on, God?* I prayed silently. *You're going to have to help. I just can't see!*

My conviction grew that Jennifer was at the church. But where? How? What did I have to go on? A gut feeling. The Bible says, "Faith is the substance of things hoped for, the evidence of things not seen." Now my own faith told me: *Believe.*

At home that night, as the ten o'clock news ended, my mind was made up. I was going back to the church. My family was afraid for my safety, but I left, taking Wayne's baseball bat with me.

I don't know when I've been as frightened as I was that night, waiting in the dark behind my office door. It was cool but my hands were sweaty on the bat. I could sense something, *someone* out there.

At 11:30 the phone rang. I leapt for it, certain someone would see the phone light up in the outer office. It was my oldest son, calling to see if I was all right. I hung up, shaking. My own breathing was so loud I was sure I'd be discovered.

I waited and waited. Well after midnight I went home.

Nothing could rid me of the feeling that Jennifer was indeed somewhere nearby. Something had to be done, and soon. Spring break started that weekend. The school would be shut down for more than a week.

Finally I devised a plan.

Thomas Mungen: *Custodian, Christ United Methodist Church*

In March 1982 I'd worked at the church for three years. It's a huge church with 4,000 members and a school attached—seven buildings in all, enough to keep me busy. At 11:30 on Thursday morning, March 18, Milton Bennett, the custodial supervisor, said we were both wanted in the pastor's office. Rev. Jerry Corlew, the interim pastor, was there. He closed the door.

"Too many unexplained things have been happening around here," the pastor said.

He was right about that. We'd been having thefts for months, especially food. The church has a weekly fellowship dinner. At first, small things were missing from the freezer, then it got to be whole turkeys or hams. The previous fall we put padlocks on the freezer. Then we put on chains and combination locks. It didn't help!

We discussed a plan Sam Drash had come up with—a still

watch, a time of just sitting quietly in the dark and watching. "Would you men be willing to do the still watch tonight?" the pastor asked. Milton and I agreed. We decided to go home and return at six. I didn't want to worry my wife, so I told her I had to work late. She didn't ask any questions, even when I asked her to drop me off two blocks from the church.

Milton and I met briefly in the custodian's room. He was going over to the fellowship hall; I would stay in the nursery, one flight below the sanctuary. Anyone coming through the church heading for the kitchen would have to pass me.

Milton took an old bedpost and I took a baseball bat. We separated quietly and slipped through the darkening church to our posts.

The nursery had a Dutch door. Between the top and bottom sections was a half inch that I could barely see through. One good thing about being in a nursery was the rocking chair. I sat down with the bat across my lap.

I was pretty sure I was waiting for teenagers. Kids who thought it was fun to steal food and leave hoax notes. Acting like that is beyond me.

At 11 o'clock a timer switched the church lights off. My eyes had hardly adjusted to the dark when I heard footsteps in the hall above me. Milton? No, it sounded like two people. I tensed up. They were coming down the steps just outside my door. There was a jangle of keys. Squinting through the nursery window, I saw a huge man and a boy. This was it.

I yelled, "Hold it! We've got you now!"

The man started running, dragging the child. When she screamed, I realized it wasn't a boy.

"Drop her! *Drop her!*" I yelled.

The man was huge. Over six feet, almost 300 pounds. He had the girl by the arm and was carrying her as easily as I carried the baseball bat. They rushed down the dark hall toward the red exit sign and crashed out into the night air.

The girl was still screaming and I started shouting too. "Milton! *Milton!*"

In the walkway outside the church the man dropped the girl and turned to me. I weigh over 240 pounds, but when I swung at him, he caught the bat and lifted me off the ground like I was a doll.

Milton came charging across the yard like a bull. The man grabbed the girl again, ran up a hill behind us and dropped her.

The three of us skirmished till the man finally took off, running toward the street. Milton and I knew we couldn't hold him by ourselves. We went to get the girl.

"I want to call my father," Jennifer Adams said.

Wayne: Jennifer told the police the kidnapper had held her captive in the church attic for four months. He had found a small area behind a series of beams and insulation that could not be seen. My dad, Thomas Mungen and even the police had stood only a few feet from the girl and her captor without seeing them. He held a knife to her throat to keep her from screaming.

They slept during the day and played board games in the attic, where he'd run in hidden electrical cords for a light and a hot plate. They roamed the church by night, eating, playing Ping-Pong and occasionally watching television. He never bothered with the locks on the freezer door, he simply took off the hinges. They showered in the bathrooms of the adjacent church houses. The kidnapper never sexually abused Jennifer, but he left her alone only long enough to go into the girls' rest room while he waited outside. It was there she'd hidden the pencil for her desperate notes.

The kidnapper was also a thief. He had a pickup truck worth of goods hidden among the attic insulation, including my dad's drill, camera, and stopwatch. Besides burglarizing many churches around town, he had burglarized houses. In fact, when he was finally caught, he had the keys to the houses of more than fifty local high school girls.

Everyone agrees Jennifer was unharmed because she was surrounded by prayers at every turn. Her classmates held prayer vigils for her. Jennifer's family never stopped praying. (In fact, Jennifer's mother didn't leave the house from the November day Jennifer disappeared until the night in March that she came home. Her mother waited for a phone call; she waited and prayed.) Perhaps most significant, Jennifer herself prayed continually. To her, God was an even stronger presence in that attic than her captor was.

But looking back, I have to say I saw something else at work too, something that has to do with faith and action. I'm proud of my dad. As far as I'm concerned, he was the hero in all this. He believed the notes were real when nobody else did, and he had the courage to act on his convictions. I'm glad our family let him go that night when we were all so afraid for him. What he did showed us the true meaning of having faith—of *knowing* that something is real even when you can't see it. For when my dad acted on that faith, the truth was revealed, and Jennifer Adams was freed.

Editor's note: *The kidnapper was caught two and a half weeks later in the crawl space of another church. He pleaded guilty and is now serving a thirty-year prison term in Tennessee.*

He had grown up in poverty and had become a drifter and a thief. When his daughter from a failed marriage rejected him, something snapped. He stole yearbooks from Memphis high schools and circled pictures of girls about his daughter's age. He broke into their houses and found spare keys, then explored different churches looking for suitable living quarters. He'd been living in Christ United Methodist for two months before the night of November 19, when he let himself into the Adamses' home and kidnapped Jennifer at knifepoint.

Since her ordeal, Jennifer has graduated from high school and college. She is currently in law school.

Members of the Flock

BY RACHEL LEFEVER, LITITZ, PENNSYLVANIA
AS TOLD TO MARTY CRISP

*This Thanksgiving story is not about
turkeys; it's about chickens.*

With Thanksgiving 1983 only two weeks away, I was counting my blessings: one good marriage, three healthy children, a farm on twelve and a half acres of green woods and rich fields, and 28,000 contented and clucking chickens laying 17,000 eggs a day. Life was good, and I was grateful—in a thank-You-God but taking-it-for-granted way.

My husband, Dave, and I had almost completed our first full year of egg farming, with a flock of birds contracted from egg suppliers R. W. Sauder, Inc. So far our hard work had paid off, and I was singing happily to myself that Sunday morning, November 13.

And then Dave came into the kitchen with a puzzled look on his face. He'd been on his morning rounds and discovered that twenty-two birds had died during the night. It's not uncommon to find five to ten dead chickens a day; that's fairly average for a flock of our size. But twenty-two?

We went to Sunday worship service, and later spent some time with our church friends. But as the day went on, I could tell Dave was uneasy, and I was too. At 9:00 P.M. Dave and I walked out hand in hand to our long white chicken-house to check the flock.

I have always loved the sound of chickens "singing," the soft and rhythmic clucking they make as they perch on their nests.

But tonight, as we stood holding our breath in the darkness, the sound we heard was a rattle, a coughing, a hacking. Dave opened one of the cages and lifted out one dead bird, then another. I began to cry.

There was no doubt: It was avian flu. This highly contagious disease of the respiratory and digestive systems can wipe out an entire flock. Our chickens had been hit. And our dreams— and our life savings—were now jeopardized by that terrible rattle.

On Monday we had forty-four dead chickens. The eggs laid by our hens were now softshelled, and some had no shells at all. The transport belt that carried the eggs became gummed and jammed, and our feet stuck to the floor where gooey yolk had dripped. The chicken feed sat uneaten in the metal trays.

On Tuesday government inspectors arrived. Our farm was placed under quarantine. Antibiotics weren't effective. We were just going to have to wait until the disease ran its course.

On Wednesday there were 439 dead chickens. It was getting harder and harder to remove them before they began rotting in their cages or in the aisles where we piled them. The whole family was up at 5:30 every day now. Our children Gwenda and Jeff, ten and thirteen, pitched right in. And Donovan, who was only five, helped load the flatbed truck; he rode along to the ditch Dave had dug on the edge of our property and helped his daddy throw dead chickens in for burial.

Thanksgiving was getting closer, but not a bone in my body was rejoicing. Day after day, the death toll mounted. On Saturday it was 1,806. The birds that were still alive hardly fluttered or made a sound at all.

A guard sat in our driveway now, enforcing the quarantine and disinfecting every vehicle that went in or out. Anyone who went in or near the chicken house had to wear a white plastic suit and scrub down before leaving the premises.

On Sunday we were up and working for two hours before church. Even though we were exhausted and every minute counted, we knew we *had* to go to church. We needed spiritual support more than ever now.

The sermon that morning was based on Habakkuk 3:17 and 18: "Although the fig tree shall not blossom, neither shall fruit be in the vines . . . the flock shall be cut off from the fold . . . Yet I will rejoice in the Lord, I will joy in the God of my salvation."

Rejoice? Thanksgiving? The Bible said it could be done, but I wasn't sure I could manage it.

At home that evening, we fell into bed exhausted yet again, but I woke up during the night to feel Dave pulling at me in his sleep. When I yipped, he woke up. "I thought you were a chicken," he mumbled.

In spite of a good middle-of-the-night laugh, on Monday morning I could barely drag myself out of bed. "I wish our chicken house would just be hit by lightning and burn down," Dave said bitterly. He had reached a point where he would almost rather watch his dreams go up in smoke than to see them rotting in the aisles. "Then we'd all move to Florida and start over."

With what? I thought wearily. We staggered out to the chicken house and started our work. It seemed especially impossible today. And just as I was thinking that, I heard the sound of cars and pickup trucks pulling into the driveway. It was my brother Nelson, with a twelve-man crew from our little Erb Mennonite Church. In forty-five minutes they did all the work that it would have taken us a whole day of struggling to do!

We were so happy for the help that I went inside and made

a batch of "apple good," a Pennsylvania Dutch treat. Even Joe, the guard, stood out in the driveway with the men in their white plastic suits and gobbled it down. For the first time since this whole thing started, I looked around at our church friends and felt a burst of genuine thankfulness.

I guess we knew it had to happen: The special Avian Flu Task Force sent by the U.S. Department of Agriculture arrived and pronounced our chickens "hot." Even a quarantine was too risky now; the entire flock of birds would have to be "depopulated" to protect other birds in the surrounding areas.

Two days before Thanksgiving the official government depopulation team arrived. It seemed we were being visited by men from outer space, as these strangers in white suits, caps and masks came to dispose of the rest of our flock—including my grandfather's prize bantam roosters.

It was almost a relief. Our poor chickens had been so sick that it hurt me to watch them. I felt so tired and overwhelmed that I got a little silly: If people with the flu eat chicken soup to feel better, I wondered, what should *chickens* with the flu eat?

"Now you folks can start your cleanup," one of the inspectors said as he was leaving. Dave and I looked around at the entire yolk-encrusted, feather-matted area. The government required that this whole area of the farm be scrubbed clean and disinfected.

For starters, we'd have to blast the walls and floors with high-pressure hoses. Then our 2,000 feet of conveyor chain and belt would have to be scraped with putty knives and scrubbed with steel wool. The lard buildup on the feed troughs had to be painstakingly scrubbed off by hand, along with the eight-foot-long manure boards under the cages. And the cages themselves had to be scoured and cleansed for all they were worth.

Barely two weeks earlier I'd counted my blessings with such satisfaction. Today the count had changed: We now had one completely empty but quite contaminated chicken house, monthly mortgage payments of $1,800, no eggs, and no income. We were about to lose everything we'd put into the farm.

And then it was Thanksgiving Day. We went to Dave's sister's for dinner. I tried to enjoy the corn pudding and apple schnitz. Everything looked delicious, but nothing tasted good to me.

"When do the church people start?" Dave's sister asked.

"Start what?"

"Cleaning up your farm."

"What?" Only then did Dave and I learn that about a hundred people from the congregation were coming over to help us.

They showed up all right, people from the church, organized by the minister, and eager to help us scour and scrape and wash. The women of the church provided ample food for the volunteers and for us.

It took days and days of hard work, but there was a lot of laughing too. Everybody helped, nobody complained. Even our mutt, Tippy, was well-behaved; I wondered if the poor dog had just given up barking at strangers since there had been so many around lately.

When the massive cleanup was over, our chicken house was as clean as any hospital operating room. But that wasn't the end of it. There were the "love gifts," money given by members of the congregation "so you can pay your bills and get started again."

On December 18, almost a month after the nightmare began, our chicken house passed inspection.

Five weeks later, on January 28, 1984, 28,000 new and healthy chickens from Perry County were delivered, and they nestled right into their spanking clean cages. When Dave and I stood in the dark that night and listened to those chickens singing peacefully, my heart was so full it just wanted to burst.

So when Thanksgiving comes around again, I will continue to count my blessings—one good marriage, three healthy children, a farm on twelve and a half acres of green woods and rich fields, 28,000 contented and clucking chickens laying 17,000 eggs a day—and most certainly our loving church family. But I'll never take these things for granted again. I'll just go on thanking God. Even for the challenges He gives us.

Part Five

*Forgiveness—
Taking the
First Step*

She's a beautiful wife and mother, and an earnest Christian, but even one of the greats of country music can run into . . .

A Break in the Music

BY BARBARA MANDRELL

ll of us who try hard to be Christians know those times when we seem to be failing, when we seem to be losing our way on His way.

Well, it happens to country singers, too. Let me tell you about one of those times in my life. But first I must explain what can happen at a typical recording session because it so well illustrates the lesson I learned.

Picture a working studio in Nashville. The singer is doing a tracking session, the first phase of recording a song. Later in the overdubbing they will add the background things like hand claps, horns, and choir. Then the performer will come back to sing the vocal again, after which the engineers will combine it all into one finished recording.

The singer, who could be me, is in the little vocal booth while the eight musicians in blue-jean-and-tee-shirt work clothes—guitarists, fiddler, French harpist, pianist, and drummer—get ready to run down a song. Eighteen microphones scattered among the group glisten under the studio's blue-green mood lights. The engineer is ready in his glassed-in control room: the producer (in my case, Tom Collins) gives the signal to start the song. But then, no recording session ever goes from start to finish without a hitch. It's just like life—there's always some unexpected problem—and in this case the band delivers the intro and the singer is just ready to come in, when *cree-yowl!*—an electronic amplifier breaks into a howling squall.

The trouble seems to be with one of the guitars. As the guitarist begins checking his equipment, the singer sits back on the tall stool in her booth and waits, and waits.

The guitar player huddles with an engineer in his rack of outboard sound equipment. The engineer calls: "I found it. Should be fixed in no time."

He holds up a small section of sound transmission wire leading from the guitar to its amplifier. Pointing to where bright copper gleams through frayed black rubber insulation, he explains that the exposed wire had touched metal, causing a short. "That's what blocked the sound from coming through," he says. They quickly switch to a new cord. "It's fixed!" he says, and the session continues.

Such a little thing, but little interruptions like that can happen in recording sessions no matter how sophisticated the equipment.

And no matter how well along the path we think we may be as Christians, there are those times when we, too, suffer a break in communication with God.

I point this out because I experienced such a break a few years ago. For several weeks something had been bothering me, and I couldn't seem to pin down what it was, or why. I had prayed time and again asking God to take away the uneasiness I was feeling, but nothing seemed to happen.

One night after rehearsal I had come home feeling particularly depressed. It had not been a good day at all. I found myself snapping at my husband Ken and being generally fretful. At bedtime I had given our baby daughter Jamie a perfunctory kiss and hardly listened to six-year-old Matthew say his prayers. Then I lay in bed unable to sleep, staring into the dark. Again I prayed, trying to listen to Him, to feel His Holy Spirit comforting and assuring me.

"Oh, Lord," I pleaded, "please give me a handle on what's bothering me."

And slowly, almost as if some invisible engineer had checked out the intricate strands of my life and suddenly called out, "I found the trouble," it came to me. It had been there all along, the resentment that had been burning within me the past weeks—*the trouble with "X."*

There's no point in telling you who "X" was, but she was someone whose friendship I'd valued and who'd said some things about me that hurt. Hurt a lot. And I was bitter.

But now, just like a spring wind blowing dark clouds away from the sun, it became clear. Just as a frayed wire can cause trouble in a sound recording studio, so had my smoldering resentment against "X" been short-circuiting my prayers.

As a serious, struggling Christian, I knew what the problem was. After all, very clearly Jesus had told us. "And whenever you stand praying, forgive. If you have anything against any one; so that your Father also Who is in Heaven may forgive you your trespasses" (Mark 11:25, 26).

Of course! I had no right to ask for peace from the One who had forgiven me so much when I would not forgive others.

"Father," I breathed, "forgive me for resenting her." And then I prayed for her well-being. I visualized her happy and smiling. And, lying there in bed, I felt at last the peace I had been seeking.

Only a few days later I saw "X" again. And do you know what? I ran up and hugged her. The amazing thing was, she hugged me back. And I'm sure she was sincere about that hug. Why ? Because I had forgiven her and somehow she had sensed this extraordinary change in me. And let me tell you, the power of forgiveness is mystifying but real!

The whole incident was such a little thing, really, a small moment so far as my life as a whole is concerned. But all of us who are trying hard to be Christians know that even little things can grow into big troubles. But when you face up to a problem and seriously take it to the Lord, there will come that wonderful time when you know "It's fixed!" and you can go on with the adventure of living.

White Candles of Forgiveness

BY JEWEL FERGUSON
FRANKFORT, INDIANA

"Come, take light," said the priest.

I stood in the midst of a group of hushed townspeople massed abut a little white church in an isolated Greek village called Zoriano. It was nearing midnight on Easter Eve. All around us were low-lying hills and, looming beyond, high mountains. Sheep's bells tinkled in the distance, and once in a while there came the soft whimpering of a baby in its mother's arms. Up the rugged pathways, out of the darkness, a few latecomers hurried to join us.

"Here," said my friend Katina, whose grandmother lived in the village, "you'll need this soon." She handed me a white candle. Then I noticed that all the people around me, mostly shepherds and farmers, simple folk in simple dress, were holding white, unlit candles. And on each person's face there was a look of great expectancy. What were they waiting for? To an American like me, the ritual was strange, but fascinating.

A bell in the church tower began to ring. I could almost feel the heavy downward pull of the long rope, and knew that with each pull each person present was silently counting the strokes—*ten . . . eleven . . .* My own pulse quickened. Then, at the moment of midnight, the church doors flung open. There was a burst of light from within, and a priest, holding a lighted candle, stepped forward. In a voice filled with exultation he proclaimed, "Christ has risen!" Katina translated quietly, thrillingly. This was the moment we had waited for, and the people responded joyfully. "Indeed, He has risen! Risen, just as He promised!"

The priest held out his candle and said, "Come, take light from Him who gives everlasting life." One by one the people moved forward. I moved with them, and one by one our candles were lighted. We shielded them from the gentle breeze of the night, waiting until the priest returned to the top step by the doorway.

The priest looked out over us and said, "Now if any has aught against a neighbor, friend, relative or enemy, go this moment and make amends. Ask forgiveness if you have wronged someone. And if they have wronged you, accept forgiveness from them. Do not carry Christ's light otherwise."

There was movement and murmuring among the crowd. Katina turned to speak to someone behind her. On my right I saw a man make his way over to another man. I didn't know what he said, of course, but when the two men embraced each other, I knew.

But what of me? I had nothing against anyone there. I had none to forgive. I was just a silent bystander. And then, somewhere from out of the deep past, I thought of something that had happened during my last year in high school. I'd confided my innermost thoughts and dreams to a close friend, but she had repeated them to others. When I found out, I was shocked, resentful; I stopped speaking to her. Later, when we attended the same college, I ignored her. Now we resided in the same town, but we never spoke.

I looked down at my candle. I knew what I had to do.

116

And I knew that Easter had come for me, too.

We made our way down the rocky path to Katina's house, and I climbed the stairs to my bedroom. From my travel bag I drew a sheet of writing paper.

"Dear Peggy . . ."

The Healing

BY ILENE MILLER
HAY LAKES, ALBERTA, CANADA

I was so confused; I couldn't remain in the house, where I might say or do something to make matters worse.

Now, as I crouched near our old chicken coop on a hill some distance away, my body trembled. The October wind was cold. I shouldn't have gone outside with wet hair and no jacket, but I wasn't thinking clearly. I was thinking only of what had just happened.

Back at the house a blue mini-bus awaited its passenger, one whom I had come to regard as a third sister and intimate friend. It was to take Maria, an eighteen-year-old Mexican girl, to another host family, presumably better than mine. It had been Maria's decision, and it was one that I could not understand.

"Who would have guessed that she was unhappy?" I asked myself. This past month I had grown to meet her expectations. Never had I been involved in so many activities; never had I felt such confidence in myself. Our shopping trips on cold rainy days, a hike with friends that almost saw us lost, movies that made us laugh until we cried, our party with Mexican food, crazy days at school, our shared confidences: All these things we had done together. Nonetheless she had been unhappy. But why had she kept this feeling to herself? Why hadn't she shared it with me?

Instead she had, through my sociology teacher, called the exchange office in New York to request that she be moved to

119

another home in our community. Her reason: My parents were too strict. I was outraged. First she had discussed it with teachers, then with neighbors, and finally New York; yet I had to find out two days later, when the New York office called our home. I felt terribly hurt.

I ground my hands together in frustration. If Maria had been displeased with me, I would have been able to clear up the whole ugly mess. But it was my parents. They were too strict, or so she thought.

This was something I couldn't deal with. I had always loved and respected my parents. Strict? I didn't think so. I hadn't any objection to asking their permission to do certain things. Sure they might say "No" sometimes, but was that bad? Didn't it show they cared? I thought it did, and I had tried in vain to explain to Maria that my parents said "No" to some of our requests because they felt responsible for us and didn't want to see us hurt. In spite of this, Maria had maintained that an eighteen-year-old should be considered an adult, independent of parental guidance.

In the distance I could hear the hum of a combine. Dad was working in the south pasture; he wouldn't know that she was leaving now. He wouldn't realize that my home-room teacher was in the house helping her to pack away her belongings. He, too, would be hurt.

And what of Mom? Her face registered pain when the teacher entered our home in the manner of a welfare worker, her main concern that of getting Maria out. Mom would be crushed; she had given this her best shot. Our home wasn't some terrible dungeon from which fair maidens were rescued!

My brothers and sisters were at school. They wouldn't realize that Maria, who had accompanied them to school, was now packing her things. They would feel bad because all of them had done their very best to help Maria fit into the family. Now she was tossing their invitation aside.

I fought back tears. I wished the sociology teacher had never gotten me involved in this stupid program. I had felt certain, with his enthusiasm, that if any problem did arise he'd be a willing mediator, but I was wrong. Today, when I needed him to sit down and talk this thing out, he couldn't be bothered. His only advice had been, "Don't feel that it is any reflection on you; these things happen to the nicest of families," and "Don't worry, just keep that chin up and you'll be okay." He hadn't even had the guts to tell me that Maria was already moving, against the wishes of my parents.

No matter how I thought about it, I *did* feel that it was a reflection on me. I knew people would think I was a terrible hostess, and then question the worth of my family. I grew angry. What right did they have to assume that things could not be worked out?

I felt tears well up in my eyes. Maria would be moving to a family who were already hosting a Mexican boy, and who had, on more than one occasion, hinted that my family didn't have the means to keep Maria happy.

I stared back at the house. My teacher was there, aiding Maria with all the cumbersome luggage she had arrived with. This would be good-bye, but I wasn't ready for it. I stood transfixed as the engine roared, then settled to a purr. Soon the doors slammed and I watched, through tears, as the little vehicle twisted out of sight.

She was gone. Tomorrow I would see her at school, and I didn't want to go. I wanted to quit. My teachers, the kids, would all know she had moved; they would wonder why. Anger seized me. How could I ever feel even a twinge of love for someone who had done this to me!

121

Slowly I began to walk to the house. Mom met me near the door; she was worried about me. There wasn't any need to worry; I wasn't going to get involved in anything anymore. I felt defeated.

Once in the house, I took some aspirins and lay down to listen to some music. Strange, but the first tune, a Paul Anka song, awakened a feeling deep inside me. Here he was singing about Jesus being our Friend, and I hadn't even thought enough to talk things over with Him. I mean, if anyone could make sense of all this, He could.

I fell into silent prayer, pouring out the whole rotten issue, asking for strength to see me through, and above all to love Maria when hate seemed so overpowering. I felt my heart grow lighter; I was sure Someone had heard me.

The next day at school, as I entered its narrow corridor, fear attacked me. "What do I do? What do I say?" a little voice begged inside me.

Maria wasn't at her locker next to mine, so I put away my things and sat down in a corner near my room. A hundred eyes were on me, waiting, watching to see what I would do.

Soon Maria approached the corner where I sat; she didn't see me. Suddenly my heart skipped a beat. She noticed me, and our eyes met. I stood up, and, to my surprise, found myself patting her on the shoulder saying, "You crazy kid, what are you up to?"

We both broke into laughter and tears. It was like yesterday had never happened. We were friends again, and for the first time I realized that if you talk things over with God, you can't go wrong.

The Untimely Phone Call

BY DORIS CRANDALL
AMARILLO, TEXAS

*Sometimes one thoughtless act can
cost you a friend.*

It was ten A.M., and I was sweeping the floor, humming, when the phone rang. *Oh, no,* I thought. I knew it was Jane. I loved her dearly, she was my closest friend and always interesting, but she just didn't know when to end a conversation! My plans for washing and waxing the floor before lunch were shot.

"Hello," I said, trying to sound cheerful.

She was so amusing that for over an hour I completely forgot about time as I listened to her stories about the washing machine breaking down, her son eating glue, and the cat knocking over her best begonia. Then I glanced at the clock. "Jane," I said hurriedly, "listen, I'm sorry to interrupt, but the doorbell just rang. Bye."

Of course there was no doorbell, but I thought it was a likely excuse. She'd never know, I reasoned, so her feelings wouldn't be hurt. Anyhow, maybe I could at least wash the floor so the whole morning wouldn't have been wasted.

Taking out the mop I wondered sardonically when she found time to do all of *her* own housework.

For the next week or so I got strangely few calls from Jane and those were unusually short. I wondered if there might be some reason for her newfound brevity, but I didn't worry about it too much: I was glad to be getting so much of my spring cleaning out of the way.

Then one day I got a long letter from my sister in Phoenix. As I read it my heart seemed to thump down to the bottom of my stomach like the end of a seesaw when your partner suddenly jumps off. She was having bad problems with her teen-aged son, who was going through a particularly difficult rebellious stage. After reading it I wanted nothing so much as to unburden myself to Jane.

Anxiously I dialed her and in grateful relief poured out all my worries about my sister and nephew. Suddenly, almost in mid-sentence, she said, "Doris, I hate to interrupt, but my doorbell just rang. See you."

She hung right up on me! How dare she! For a moment I just stood there, stunned, holding the phone in midair. I almost wept with anger. Then, in a burst of energy, I flew into my housework. I began furiously attacking the hall closet— now was a great time to really clean it up, from top to bottom! I jerked some boxes off a shelf a bit too forcefully and they came toppling down, hundreds of papers scattering over the floor like giant confetti.

It was more than I could take. Sitting on the floor, I started to weep in exasperation. But my tears were cut short when I recognized what the papers were—little Scripture cards that Mama had used when teaching Sunday school. She was dead now, and the cards were precious reminders to me of her classes. I had taken special pride in memorizing the verse on every card. As I began gathering them up I was transported back to the makeshift schoolroom in the small country church we attended. There was Mama standing before the class, holding a card and telling us about it, simply and plainly. She believed in absolutely every word.

I looked at the card I held in my hand. In orange crayon I had written: "The Golden Rule." It read: "Always treat others as you would like them to treat you; that is the law and the prophets."

I just sat there for a few minutes in the midst of scattered papers, staring at the card. Of course! If I didn't want a friend hanging up on me, what made me think I could get away with the same behavior?

I remembered Mama saying, "No one ever outgrows the Golden Rule."

I knelt on the closet floor, feeling humble and ashamed. I bowed my head and prayed: "Heavenly Father. You know I've got things in a mess. I'm really sorry. Help me straighten things out with Jane."

Just then a tremendous desire to apologize to her came over me. I felt it so strongly, I jumped up and ran to the phone.

"Jane," I said, before she could even say hello. "I have to ask your forgiveness. I was mad at you for hanging up on me, but I know I used the same excuse on you—and it was a lie."

"Oh, Doris, I'm so glad you called," she said. "I'm sorry, too. I was so hurt you'd use that old line on me about the doorbell ringing. I guess I was trying to get even by using it on you, too. It wasn't very neighborly of me."

So we both forgave and apologized. I told her about how I'd found the Scripture card and we agreed to put the Golden Rule into our friendship and be more honest with each other.

Now, whenever one of us calls the other, the first question is "How long have you got?" Whether it's an hour or a minute, we honor each other's schedule. And I've stuck that old Scripture card, creased and worn, grimy from all the little hands that held it, on the bulletin board by the phone. Mama was right: You don't grow out of the Golden Rule; you grow into it.

It's Hard to
Say I'm Sorry

BY VICKI JO HALL
CARROLLTON, ILLINOIS

We were very good at hurting each other.
Could we be just as good at forgiving?

That summer, back in 1972, had started out very well. I had my summer planned and was looking forward to a busy but exciting summer vacation. One of the activities I looked forward to the most was the Community Chorus preparations for an elaborate show-business production in the fall. That's where I met Barry.

His parents were in the chorus and had urged Barry to join. We girls were in for a treat because he was just dreamy. We could hardly wait for each rehearsal, so we could gaze at him. After a while, I began to hear that he liked me too. He had told a few people, hoping it would conveniently get back to me. Boy, was I in seventh heaven!

And so I began to know the meaning of first love. After each rehearsal, I'd take off on cloud nine. But sometimes first love can be bittersweet.

Toward the end of the summer, things changed. Barry would sometimes act as if I didn't exist; other times he'd act like he usually did and we'd have fun. I was getting a little confused.

Even though we weren't actually dating, because he didn't have a driver's license, I invited him to a hay ride our church

127

was having. We were both disappointed when we discovered he would be away in Pennsylvania on a trip with his parents. But he reassured me that he wanted a rain check on the invitation.

In the meantime I met Russ. He was in the band that played for our chorus production. He was very nice, and we soon began to correspond and see each other occasionally. But Barry very much lingered in my thoughts.

About that time, a movie came to town that was church-sponsored. I remembered what Barry had said about the rain check, so I asked him if he wanted to go. In reply, he wrote me a letter saying he couldn't go, but that wasn't all. The letter was filled with things that proceeded to tear my world apart. There was another girl. He described her in detail and proclaimed his great love for her. Even more disappointing was his conceit; he thought I would be crushed, and he seemed to enjoy it. He said he knew that I would always love him because he "could see it in my eyes."

I was alternately very sad and then very mad. My heart told me not to let him get away with this. So I collected my thoughts and wrote him a letter, wishing him all kinds of good luck with his new girl. I proceeded to describe Russ, telling about his many honors and how much I liked him. I ended the letter by telling Barry not to worry about me as I really hadn't liked him for a while because I found his mirror to be too much competition.

As I look back on it now, I have to laugh at how dramatic we both were.

After that we each became aloof, irritating each other at every opportunity. I had accomplished my goal; I had hurt *him* deeply, too. But we had started a vicious circle, and Barry now had to dream up more ways to hurt me.

Then came the final blow.

It was music-contest time, and one of my entries was a difficult clarinet solo by Bach. I had practiced for four months. I was dreading my time with the judge, and as I walked into the contest room, there sat Barry. As I started to play, my fingers shook over the keys with the difficulty of the solo. But Barry gave me the most humiliating of revenges as he deliberately set out to distract me from my music. I began to fall apart, though somehow I made it through to the end. Tears started down my cheeks as I ran from the room, feeling very much like a fool. My months of hard practice had gone down the drain.

My friends were so mad, they all wanted to go to Barry's solo and mess *him* up. But suddenly, I realized that two wrongs don't make a right and I persuaded them to dismiss the idea.

Then I learned that Barry was proud to have caused me to fail and was bragging about his accomplishment!

From that time on, we didn't speak to each other at all and went out of our way to avoid one another. Unavoidably, we were thrown together on many occasions, which made the resentment more painful.

Our battle continued for a whole year and as time wore on, I learned from our mutual music teacher, that Barry was sorry for what he had done, but could not bring himself to ask for my forgiveness. *What a waste bitterness is!* I thought. *It's like acid that eats at its own container.*

Meanwhile, the Lord was helping me to feel differently about all this. I didn't feel hate toward Barry anymore and I almost had to remind myself not to speak to him. I began to realize that as a Christian I should practice what I had believed all these years—that forgiveness can be there, just for the asking. I knew that if I asked for Barry's forgiveness and offered mine, no matter what happened, at least my heart would be at peace.

I arranged a meeting through our music teacher. The feud had troubled her greatly and she was just as anxious to see it end. I prayed hard that God would help me to say the right things.

When Barry walked into the room, he looked like he was about to be executed. I began slowly, with God as my guide, to ask Barry to forgive me for all the things I had done to hurt him. I told him that I forgave him for all the things he had done to me during the year even though he hadn't asked for my forgiveness.

"Isn't a year long enough to be enemies?" I continued. "Isn't it about time we ended this cold war?"

He walked across the room silently, and I thought my efforts had been in vain.

Then he turned toward me, and I could see the relief flooding his face as he said, "You don't know how many times I've tried to say, 'I'm sorry.'" Suddenly we were talking and laughing in the excitement of being friends once again.

Barry and I are still good friends to this day, and I treasure that friendship for all it cost us. He's different now, and so am I. We both did a lot of growing up during that time. And we learned a valuable lesson—that unless someone takes that first difficult step, the circle of revenge and bitterness will never be broken. That's something I'll remember all my life.

The Grudge

BY DON HAZELL
DURANT, OKLAHOMA

If I was right—and I knew I was—
why did I feel so wrong?

J ames Bowers ran a hand through his dark, curly hair. He wasn't smiling as he tossed a folded *Southeastern* on my desk.

"Did you see that?" he asked.

I knew what article in the Southeastern State University newspaper James had in mind: a column that, in effect, called for his firing. He was coaching a losing basketball team at our college, where winning had been the tradition for many years. We were currently last in a ten-team conference, and James' job was on the line. The administration, the alumni, the community, the students—everyone wanted a winner.

I liked winning, too. A biology professor at Southeastern, I'd been named faculty athletic representative. The sports program was important to me—but not as important to me as James was. He was my friend. We played golf together and bowled on the same team. I knew his wife and four children. And I knew the pressure he was feeling. In the last game, I'd watched him explode in crimson fury over an official's call. It wasn't like him.

"Well, this season's almost over," I consoled.

"Yes," James said. "I've already got the message, though. It's next year—or else."

"Do we have any prospects?" I asked.

"Well, yes," James replied. "I'm recruiting a junior college player who was All-American this year. If he comes to Southeastern, he could be the difference between last and first place for our team."

So, a few months later, I was glad to learn that one member of my fall biology class was six-foot-eight Billy Collins.* But I wasn't glad for long.

Billy was a very poor student. He might have passed the course if he had made any effort. But he skipped class repeatedly, and flunked every test. I offered to tutor Billy privately, but he wasn't interested. And I guess the warnings that came through James had no effect on his "star" player.

At the close of the semester, right before the start of basketball season, Billy wasn't even close to passing. Yet, if he failed, he would be scholastically ineligible to play. I not only wanted our college to have a winning team, but I knew that losing Billy could cost James his job. It was a tough decision for me, but there seemed to be no choice except to flunk Billy. And I did.

A few days later, walking along the sidewalk in front of the Administration Building, I passed right by James. He turned his head away, I shrugged it off. But a few days later as I approached him in similar fashion, he crossed over to the other side of the street. This wasn't my imagination, James didn't want to see me. I was losing a friend.

Things went from bad to worse. The team had another losing season, and James was relieved of his coaching duties.

Now the situation between him and me even involved our families. When my wife, Koula, and I passed Robbie Bowers in a local supermarket, she wouldn't acknowledge our greeting. On another occasion, I was watching an American Legion

*Name has been changed.

132

baseball game when I spotted one of James' sons at Southside Park.

"Hi, Alan," I called.

"Don't speak to me," he snapped back, "because I'm not about to talk to you."

To him, of course, I was the disloyal friend who'd cost his father his coaching job. But suddenly I was very bitter. After all, James was still teaching special education courses at the college; he wasn't unemployed. And I had only been doing my job when I flunked Billy Collins. I was in the right. If James couldn't see that, it was his fault.

Once I told myself that, it was easy to justify a lot of things. James wouldn't speak to me; all right, I wouldn't speak to him. He wanted to avoid me; fine, I would shun him, too.

And that's the way it was. I saw James on campus, I saw him at faculty meetings. Once or twice I saw him on the golf course, as we played in separate foursomes now. Each time, I said nothing.

Months passed this way, I hated to admit it to myself, but I wasn't happy. My conscience wouldn't rest.

"I don't understand it, Lord," I'd pray. "I just did my job, I didn't do anything wrong. It's James' fault. So why should I feel bad?"

These prayers never left me satisfied.

Nearly two years after my friendship with James had broken up, Christians in our community began preparing for an area-wide evangelistic crusade. Part of the preparation for this event was a week of counselor training, which my wife and I attended. James and his wife also came to these sessions: We belonged to different denominations, but were all active church members. Still, it bothered me that we could be sitting there at the same gatherings, when there was such a lack of

Christian feeling in our personal lives. And nothing was about to change. Koula and I sat on the opposite side of the meeting hall from James and Robbie Bowers. I justified the continuing friction, telling my wife, "Well, I know I'm not to blame for it."

The training sessions went on for a few days. At the final meeting, just before we were ready to participate in the crusade and share our Christian faith with others, one of the crusade leaders spoke to us.

"You know how glad we are to have you all with us," he said. "And we'd like to be able to do something for each of you. At the close of the meeting, I hope we'll all take care of our personal needs, for salvation and rededication. We all want to get rid of any sin or any kind of barrier that might hinder our effectiveness as counselors during the crusade."

Suddenly, it struck me. All the bitterness and pain I'd felt over the past two years—it didn't come from James. Here I was supposed to be a follower of Christ, who forgave sinners *even before they asked Him to.* Yet I'd been so convinced of my own righteousness that I'd waited almost two years for James to make the first move. And by letting so much ill-feeling take over during that time, I'd poisoned my own spirit.

"I'm sorry, Lord," I prayed sincerely. "Please help me start over."

At the close of the meeting I rose, took a couple of steps toward the center aisle from my seat on the left side of the auditorium, and started to walk forward. Then I saw him.

Coming over from the right side—excusing himself as he moved past people, making his way to the center aisle just as I had done—was James Bowers.

He looked up, and we caught each other's eyes. In each of us, the other saw an awkward, pained look caused by those many months of silence. And, miraculously, the look changed from pain to understanding, from understanding to hope. In a moment we were wrapping our arms around each other, thanking the Lord for bringing us together again.

"Life's too short for hating," James said. And no matter what would follow, I knew this particular spiritual crusade was already a success.

It didn't take us long to get things back to normal. A short time after that night, the Hazells and the Bowerses held a two-family picnic outing. We had an opportunity, after all that lost time, to get reacquainted and to catch up on all the happenings in our families and in our lives.

"You know, it's great that we don't have to be strangers any more," Koula told Robbie Bowers. Then both wives turned to James and me. "Say, whose fault was all this, anyway?" they questioned jokingly.

My reply was serious: "That" I said, "is the question we both decided to stop asking."

The Old Bureau

BY HAZEL F. ZIEMAN
WHITTIER, CALIFORNIA

*It's hard to believe that an old piece of
furniture could kill a friendship.*

I would never have believed an old bureau could have caused
such bitterness between Barbara and me. Next-door neighbors for six years, we were close friends, one or the other
always on hand if needed.

But then came the sale. Distant cousins of mine were moving out of state. They had to get rid of much of their furniture.

"She's letting several of her lovely pieces go," I told Barbara.
"One of them is a bureau of solid walnut, over a hundred years
old. You must go with me to the sale."

"Always trying to get me interested in antiques," Barbara
laughed. "All right, I'll go," she agreed.

"And be prepared to buy something this time," I urged her.

My grandmother had told me how great-great Uncle Ned
had built the bureau, had carved the oak-leaf handles himself,
had taken it across the country in a covered wagon. I'd admired the bureau many times, not dreaming I'd have the
chance to own it.

At my cousin's suggestion, we went over very early the day of
the sale, so we could choose any of the things we wished. My
cousin was on the phone when we got there, but her husband
began to show us around. I was looking at some old pieces of
silver, waiting to tell my cousin I'd take the bureau, when
Barbara walked up and said, "Well, I did it. I bought something."

137

"Good! Show me what you got," I said. She took me over and pointed to the bureau. "Not my bureau!" I must have shouted, for Barbara backed off, looking shocked and hurt.

"*Your* bureau! I thought that's what you wanted me to buy," she said.

I must have gone temporarily insane. I said some awful things to Barbara: How she *knew* I wanted the bureau more than anything in the world. How I thought she was my friend. How I hated her for this. Barbara ran out of the house. I never did find out how she got home.

I felt sick inside. Several times in the next few days, I started to go over to apologize. When I finally did get up my nerve, Barbara saw me coming and ran from her yard into the house. I didn't know what to do, so I went back home. Weeks passed without our talking with each other.

One day, we unexpectedly came face to face in the supermarket. Both of us stammered "hello," but that was all. Gradually the whole thing began to look pretty ridiculous to me. I'd got us into this mess and I'd get us out.

So I went over and rang Barbara's door bell. "This whole thing is silly," I said.

"I've known that for a long time," she answered. But her voice was icy, and she didn't smile.

I choked up and turned away. How could she make it so hard for me?

The next month, at PTA meeting, Barbara and I were both assigned to the planning committee for our annual spring festival. I thanked God for another chance. Maybe Barbara would have changed her mind by now and be willing to meet me halfway. But when the committee met, she didn't show up. "Isn't Barbara coming?" I asked the chairman.

"Said she couldn't possibly serve. Personal reasons."

138

Well! I thought. *That's certainly a slap in the face!*

A strange ugliness settled inside me. It squeezed my throat muscles, slithered into my head, until the pressure gave me a headache.

When my cousin had phoned to say Barbara didn't want the bureau and when would I like to pick it up, I had told her to take one of the other offers she had on it, that I never wanted to see it again. And now I hated it more than ever.

One day I was reading my Bible for a few minutes after the children left for school. I'd got into the book of Ephesians and was starting the fourth chapter. A couple of lines pricked at me.

"Accept life with humility and patience, making allowances for one another" (Phillips translation).

I read that passage over and over. "Making allowances . . . because you love one another." Hadn't I tried to love Barbara with Christian love? Then I put the Bible down and kneeled beside my bed in desperation.

"God," I prayed, "this is such a little thing, but it's got so terribly big inside of me. All I can feel for Barbara is resentment. I've tried to love her, but it just doesn't seem to work. I know You have enough love. If I could just borrow from You for a while, I'm sure the feeling will come to me."

A great sense of relief filled me. I moved happily through my household routine and felt a joyous anticipation for my husband and children's homecoming and our family dinner, for the countless little things of the next few days.

But God wasn't through with me. A couple of days later, as I was reading on in Ephesians, I came across these words: "If you are angry, be sure that it is not out of wounded pride or bad temper" (Ephesians 4:26).

No wonder I hadn't been able to feel Christian love. All this time I'd been blaming Barbara for refusing to do her part. It began to be clear that God expected something more of me. If His love was going to show through me, it needed some sort of action on *my* part!

I was going to have to demonstrate my feelings. Several times that week, I called "hello" to Barbara across the backyard fence. By the end of the week, she answered my greeting.

Open house at school was coming up the next Tuesday, so I went over to her house that morning.

"Barbara, I'm going down to open house tonight. Won't you ride with me?"

She hesitated, giving me a long puzzled look. Silently I prayed, *God bless you, Barbara,* and I tried to beam a feeling of love toward her. Aloud I said, "I'd really like to have you."

I'm sure she felt something, for she smiled suddenly. "All right," she said.

Every time I was with Barbara, I beamed love toward her. It wasn't long until our old relationship had returned.

I know those verses from Ephesians by heart now. They taught me that what I can do is pretty limited. But what God can do through me, if I let Him, is something else again.

Part Six

Friendship Connects

"Margaret Patrick Meet Ruth Eisenberg"

BY MARGARET PATRICK, ENGLEWOOD, NEW JERSEY
AND BY RUTH EISENBERG, CLIFFSIDE PARK, NEW JERSEY
AND BY THE EDITORS OF GUIDEPOSTS

A most unusual arrangement

We're going to tell you the stories of two women, two very different women. One of them, Margaret Patrick, seventy-four, is tall and stately and soft-spoken. The other, Ruth Eisenberg, eighty-five, is short and round and feisty. Margaret Patrick wears soft-colored fabrics made into tailored suits; Ruth Eisenberg wears dresses in colorful prints of peacock feathers or geometric patterns. Margaret Patrick shies away from public attention; Ruth Eisenberg feels quite comfortable addressing an audience on stage. For all of her life, Margaret Patrick has felt close to God and close to music; for much of hers, Ruth Eisenberg felt close to neither. Whatever could bring such opposites—one, a black woman, the other, white—together? That is what we intend to tell.

Margaret's Story

I grew up in Harlem, and as a young child I dreamed of playing the piano. When I was eight, my father found a neighborhood teacher, and my lessons began. We could not afford a piano. I "practiced" at Mother's sewing machine. Even so, I learned quickly, and I felt from the beginning that God had given me this talent.

When my teacher saw what an ardent pupil I was, she urged my father to buy a piano. It was a great sacrifice, but two

143

months later, there it stood in the center of our living room! It was the most important piece of furniture in our house.

From that day on, music became everything to me. Pounding out the same songs over and over, I'd ignore my mother's call.

"Mar-r-rgaret, supper's ready."

Then, in frustration, she would come and get me: "Margaret, didn't you hear me, girl? Get off that bench this minute. You've got to eat!"

And so it went, day after day, year after year. Every few cents I could save would go toward buying sheet music. God made me hungry for music.

Soon, people were asking me to play—first at Sunday school, then during exercise class in gym, later for our church choir. And finally, churches in New York and New Jersey began calling on me when they needed an organist.

In 1929 I graduated from the Martin Smith Conservatory of Music in Manhattan, and I still have the gold medal they awarded me for piano and theory. In the years that followed, I hammered away on the keyboard for singers, for orchestras, for violinists. Never alone, if I could help it—I didn't like the attention. I just didn't enjoy the spotlight.

Music was my love, and so was Leonard. We married in 1934, and five babies blessed our home. As soon as they could sit on the piano bench, I was teaching them—Dolores, Leona, Leroy, Carol, and Carmen.

We moved to the Bronx, and I played for the Saint Augustine Church choir for thirty-three years. Some of those years I had to nurse and feed and shower and dress Leonard, who'd had a stroke in 1969. Music helped me through the hardships, through the weariness. I could always turn to the keyboard; that was the Lord's gift to me.

But then, one cold January Sunday in 1982, I phoned our

minister: "Hello, Pastor Rollins. I won't be able to play at rehearsal this morning."

I didn't explain that something inside told me not to go out that morning.

After hanging up the phone, I felt weak, my breathing came in gasps. Frightened, I called my sister, Catherine. "I can hardly breathe," I struggled to say. "Please hurry!"

I was sixty-nine and having a heart attack. That night, in the hospital, I had another, and then, days later, I had a stroke.

I couldn't move. I couldn't speak. The doctors didn't expect me to live. But as I lay in that stark hospital room, I silently rejoiced at being alive. "Thank You, God, thank You, God!" was in my mind each passing day. I know He heard my thoughts.

Gradually I recovered. I regained my speech, and in time I returned to my house on a wooded road in Englewood, New Jersey. I could no longer take care of Leonard; we needed a nurse and an aide to help us through each day. And when I finally could sit down at my piano, there was not enough strength in my right hand to play the keys. The fingers would not bend and flex.

With my left hand, I worked the keyboard in a lonely search for simple tunes. "God, You've saved my life and I'm grateful," I told Him. "But, Lord, I no longer have music. What am I to do, Lord?" Yes, I was happy to be alive, but grieving over my loss.

Ruth's Story

Our home had a piano, and when I was eight, my parents signed me up for music lessons. How I hated that piano! No, of course I wouldn't practice!

"Ruth," my mother would call, "Ruth, where are you? I want you to practice your piano lesson before dinner."

"Oh, Mo-o-o-ther, not today, please!"

"Yes, Ruth, now!"

I'd wail and stumble over the simplest tunes, and yell, "It's too hard. I can't do it!"

Finally acknowledging my lack of interest and talent, Mother and Dad discontinued my lessons. "A waste of money," they agreed.

I had no feeling for music. Concerts were boring; I avoided them. But then, at the age of twenty-two, I married Jacob. He made his living by writing textbooks for piano teachers.

"Ruth, why don't you become my student?" he asked. He'd been asking me this for months. "You could test the methods that I write about."

"No, Jacob, I don't have time for the piano."

He persisted.

I said no.

And then something interesting happened. Jacob began to surprise me by doing the housework whenever I sat down at the piano. The more I practiced, the more work he did.

His plan worked in two ways. One, of course, was that his doing the housework made me *want* to practice. But also, I was so impressed and delighted with his efforts to help me out that I grew determined to please him too. So I decided that, for Jacob, I'd keep plugging away at the piano.

I did, and soon I became Jacob's star, traveling with him on tours across the country to play in front of large audiences. In time I learned to love the attention, the applause. The spotlight was the place for me!

Under Jacob's careful schooling, I finally learned to feel and love the compositions of Mendelssohn, Chopin, Bach, and other great masters. Then, in 1964, Jacob died. Hour after hour, I sat over the keyboard playing the music he had taught me. That was my salvation. You see, I had no faith. God had not been a part of my world.

For years I volunteered to play the piano at senior citizen homes. It was a way of spreading the joy of music that Jacob had left with me. It also eased my loneliness.

Then, one hot August day in 1982, I collapsed in my apartment. I had had a stroke. For two days I lay helpless on the floor, drifting in and out of consciousness. Weak and scared, I wondered how long I'd last.

Finally, I heard a key turn in the lock, the voice of a neighbor and other voices, the phone ringing. It seems such a nightmarish blur—being rushed to the hospital, and all.

When I recovered, I was devastated. The left side of my body was paralyzed.

"Mrs. Eisenberg," the doctors told me, "you'll be needing a wheelchair—"

"No!" I cut them short.

My daughter, Jackie, took me to her home in Connecticut for several months before taking me back to my apartment in Cliffside Park, New Jersey. How cruel it seemed: Music had become the most important thing in my life, and now all I could do was sit and brood bitterly over the piano that I could no longer play. I stroked the keys longingly with my right hand, while my left hand lay limp and useless on my knee.

Eventually I forced myself to attend an exercise-therapy class at the Southside Senior Center for Independent Living located in Englewood. I used those visits, however, to commiserate with other ailing people; and if any stalwart soul suggested trusting in the Lord, I'd snap back, "If God existed, He wouldn't have done this to me!"

The Story of Margaret and Ruth

In the spring of 1983 Margaret Patrick arrived at the Southeast Senior Center for Independent Living to begin her physical therapy. As Millie McHugh, a long-time staff member, introduced Margaret to people at the center, she noticed the look of pain in Margaret's eyes as she gazed at the piano.

"Is anything wrong?" asked Millie.

"No," Margaret said softly. "It's just that seeing a piano brings back memories. Before my stroke, music was everything to me." Millie glanced at Margaret's useless right hand as the black woman quietly told some of the highlights of her music career.

Suddenly Millie was saying, "Wait right here. I'll be back in a minute." She returned moments later, followed closely by a small, white-haired woman in thick glasses. The woman used a walker.

"Margaret Patrick," said Millie, "meet Ruth Eisenberg." Then she smiled. "She too played the piano, but like you, she's not been able to play since her stroke. Mrs. Eisenberg has a good right hand, and you have a good left, and I have a feeling that together you two can do something wonderful."

"Do you know Chopin's Waltz in D flat?" Ruth asked. Margaret nodded.

Side by side, the two sat on the piano bench. Two healthy hands—one with long, graceful black fingers, the other with short, plump white ones—moved rhythmically across the ebony and ivory keys. Since that day, they have sat together over the keyboard hundreds of times—Margaret's helpless right hand around Ruth's back, Ruth's helpless left hand on Margaret's knee, while Ruth's good hand plays the melody and Margaret's good hand plays the accompaniment.

Their music has pleased audiences on television, at churches and schools, and at rehabilitation and senior-citizen centers. And on the piano bench, more than music has been shared by these two. For it was there, beginning with Chopin and Bach and Beethoven, that they learned they had more in common than they ever dreamed—both were great-grand-mothers and widows (Margaret's husband died in 1985), both had lost sons, both had much to give, but neither could give without the other.

Sharing that piano bench, Ruth heard Margaret say, "My music was taken away, but God gave me Ruth." And evidently some of Margaret's faith has rubbed off on Ruth as they've sat side by side these past five years, because Ruth is now saying, "It was God's miracle that brought us together."

And that is our story of Margaret and Ruth, who now call themselves Ebony and Ivory.

149

The Man Who Wanted to Go Home

BY JIMMY GUPTON
CHARLOTTE, NORTH CAROLINA

*When you're ninety-three and alone,
you begin to wonder if you're just too
old for Christmas.*

nother Christmas coming . . . toy commercials and holiday specials on television. And here I was, an old man spending another evening in front of the tube.

Why, Lord? I asked Him for the thousandth time. *Why won't You just go ahead and take me home?*

I'd been a Christian all my life and figured the Almighty didn't mind my taking a familiar tone with Him. *Ninety-three years is long enough on this earth. I've lived a full life, and I can't see where I'm much good to You or anyone else anymore.*

When my wife was alive it was different. But Bess had been gone now seven years, and lately it was getting harder to go through the motions. Christmas, for example. I hadn't even bothered to get the big silver tree out of the box in the attic this year. It was a pretty thing, but attaching 150 branches was a big job. After my eyes went bad, I'd had to take an ice pick to feel for the holes. With only me here, why bother?

A rock group came on the screen to sing "Jingle Bells." *You see, Lord, I'm not going to be able to take care of this place much longer, and You know I don't want to go somewhere else.* My two sons and their families kept asking me to move in with one of them, but

151

I'm a stubborn kind of fellow. I liked it here, liked my independence.

This past year, though . . . It was a small house, but it was getting to be too much. The roof was leaking, the wallpaper peeling. *Why can't I just come home, Lord, and not fool with an interim move?*

On the screen now were pictures of the Salvation Army shelter in downtown Charlotte, part of a series on the homeless at Christmas. "There are over two hundred women sleeping here tonight," an announcer said, "out of work and out of hope." I sure felt sorry for those people. But I hardly had enough money to cover my own expenses, much less make a donation. At about ten o'clock I switched off the set, turned off the lights and said my usual prayers before climbing into bed.

Instead of falling asleep, though, I kept seeing those women at the shelter. I'd always given to the poor when I was able. Surely it was someone else's turn now. But that news report wouldn't let me alone. There were those women needing help. Just like me, I thought.

I sat up in bed. What if two needy folks were to put their needs together? What if one of these women were to move in here, take care of the house in exchange for a place to live?

The next morning I telephoned the shelter. "If you're serious, Mr. Gupton," the manager said, "I'll ask around."

A few days after Christmas he called back: "Would you consider taking in a married couple?"

"Well, now . . ." I hadn't counted on *two* people. "It's such a small house," I apologized. "The spare room's barely big enough for one."

"What I was thinking," the man went on, "was that the wife could keep house and the husband could look after the yard.

As for the size of the room, I'm sure anything with a door on it would look like a palace to them right now."

The manager paused a moment to let this sink in. "I think I've got the perfect couple. Tony and Pam Davis."

Both Davises had lost their jobs. Unable to meet rent payments, they'd been evicted from their home, and ended up sleeping at the shelter at night and job hunting during the day. "It's hard to impress an employer, wearing wrinkled clothing, having no permanent address."

"Send them on over," I said. "We'll give it a try."

It looked as though it was going to work. Pam was a little shy at first, but before the week was out we were chatting like old friends. She told me she'd been a waitress while Tony worked as a carpet installer, until both places of employment went out of business the same month. With downcast eyes she described what it had been like to be in a Salvation Army shelter at Christmastime.

It was nice to have someone keeping house, cooking meals, taking care of the yard again. Wonderful to have them care enough to escort me to the senior citizens' center, to drive me to church.

About three months after they'd come, though, Pam said she needed to talk to me. The two of us had just finished lunch; Tony had found a job with another carpet installation company and was gone during the day.

"I don't know how to say this, Mr. Gupton," she began.

Oh, no! I thought. *She's going to tell me they're moving out now that Tony's working.*

Pam got up and started piling dishes in the sink. "I know I should have told you in the beginning," she said, "but I was afraid you wouldn't let us stay—and you might want us to leave after you hear this. But I can't put off telling you any longer ..."

She twisted the dishrag in her hands. "You see, I . . . I'm . . ." She lifted her dark eyes to stare into mine. "I'm going to have a baby."

So that was it! "Well, you're right about one thing," I said. "I hadn't counted on three of you, that's for sure." She turned away, looking down at the sink. "But I certainly can't let you go back on the streets," I assured her. "Not with a baby coming." I tried to keep my voice calm, but my mind was shouting, *A baby! Where will we put a baby?*

"I know there's not much room here," Pam said as if reading my thoughts. "But if we move the dresser out of our room, I'm sure we could squeeze a small crib in, and I'll try to keep the baby quiet so it won't disturb you too much."

The months flew by. Pam shifted the tiny room around to sandwich a crib between the bed and the wall, bought diapers and bottles, and began a whirlwind of painting and wallpapering all over the house.

And before I knew it, a redheaded baby girl named Sabrina arrived. Pam tried to keep her quiet and out of my way as much as possible. Soon she was three months old, then five months old, and then it was the middle of December—almost Christmas again.

I was sitting in the living room one evening reading the second chapter of Luke as I always did at this time of year: "And she brought forth her firstborn Son," I read, "and laid Him in a manger; because there was no room for them in the inn" (v. 7).

That must have saddened God, I thought, feeling pretty good that I'd found room for the Davis family, though in some ways it had been an inconvenience. Even as I thought about the crowded inn, though, I knew that wasn't the point of the story. What God had wanted, far more than a room at the inn, was

154

for people to open their hearts and make room for His Son.

Perhaps that's what he'd been trying to get me to do. Sure, I'd made room for the Davises in my house, but maybe God had been trying to get me to make room in my heart.

The winter wind was beating at the old windows, seeping round the newspapers Pam had stuffed into the cracks. I got up and stoked the fire in the wood stove, had to keep the place warm for the baby. *You know,* I told myself, *if we slid the couch back against the wall, I believe there'd be room for a playpen in here. Can't keep a growing child cooped up in a bedroom.*

I walked over to the stairs. "Tony! Pam!" I called.

"What is it, Mr. Gupton?" Tony asked, hurrying down.

"Is something wrong?" said Pam, following behind him, alarm in her eyes.

"You bet something's wrong," I said. "Here it is, almost Christmas, and we don't have a tree up!"

"We thought about that," Tony admitted. "But trees are so expensive."

"That's so," I agreed. "But I happen to know where there's a beautiful tree just waiting to be put up. It's in a box in the attic now, but when it's standing tall and grand with the colored lights beaming across its silver branches, you never saw anything so pretty in all your life. With a child in the house, we've got to have a Christmas tree!"

Tony and Pam raced up the rickety stairs to the attic and dragged down the bulky box. Pam unpacked the branches; I fluffed out the tinsel "needles" and passed them to Tony to insert in the holes. It was fun doing it together. I coached Tony as he set the tree in the revolving stand I'd made out of an old TV antenna many years before. Then I switched on the multicolored floodlight and sat back to enjoy their ooh's and aah's as the tree started to turn like a silver ballerina.

About that time, we heard a hungry wail from upstairs. Pam ran up and brought Sabrina down. She looked surprised, but pleased, when I motioned for her to hand the baby to me while she went off to the kitchen to heat a bottle. We sat there, eyeing each other silently. I felt kind of awkward. After all, it had been some time since I'd conversed with a young child.

Sabrina studied my face intently, and for a moment I thought she was going to cry. But instead she broke into a laugh and reached a chubby little hand toward my cheek. I laughed too when I realized she was trying to catch the fleeting reflections from the tree. The touch of her hand made me think of another child, born on Christmas so many years ago.

I looked at Tony, arranging candles in the window, listened to Pam humming a carol out in the kitchen. And I whispered a prayer to the One who has our times in His keeping.

Thank You, Lord, for letting me see another Christmas . . . for leaving me here though I fussed and fretted. Sometimes it takes a baby to remind an old man what Your world is all about.

The Good Connection

BY WALTER HARTER
ST. AUGUSTINE, FLORIDA

*How did a telephone help bring
a man back to life?*

Often if you stand too close to a painting it appears to be composed of meaningless globs of color. When you view it from a distance, however, each brush stroke is seen to be important to all the others, and completes the picture.

So, too, with even the simple events of our lives. Each one alone might seem to have no meaning, but at a distance there appears to be *something* that has connected them into a meaningful pattern. I'm sure that's what happened to my life.

A long time ago, after almost fifteen years in New York City, I returned to Bethlehem, Pennsylvania. I'd had my fill of life in the Big City, and I missed my hometown. Also my parents were growing older and needed me. As a young man I'd discovered adventure in New York. But now I was older and wiser, and I was sure adventure and opportunity could be found anywhere. I also had a plan.

I knew my handicap (polio) would still make it difficult to find a regular job, so my plan involved trying to start a small business of my own. I had always dabbled in photography, developing and printing my pictures in makeshift arrangements in bathrooms and kitchens, but now I wanted to do it properly.

I'd managed to save a little money, and with it I constructed

157

a small darkroom, complete with a secondhand enlarger, in a corner of my parents' basement. I had just enough money left to pay my parents a modest board and to assemble some supplies.

For the next few months I took pictures of the children in my neighborhood. I worked almost constantly, taking pictures, then developing and printing them in my darkroom. I also studied every book about photography I could obtain from the public library. At the end of that time I had produced an album of quite good photographs.

I began by knocking on doors. If there were children in the family, I showed my samples and offered to take pictures of them at no charge. In a few days (always in the evenings when *both* parents were at home) I'd return with proofs of the pictures. If the parents liked any of them I'd make enlargements, according to a modest price list. If the parents didn't like any of the proofs, I'd thank them for their time and leave.

Luckily most of the pictures were liked, and soon my small business began to grow. I could have done more, but a great amount of time was wasted knocking on doors where there were no children. It was then that a chain of events started that was to affect my life and the lives of others.

One day I knocked on a door and heard a voice call, "Come in." When I entered the small living room, I noticed at once the absence of toys or other signs of small children. But I did see a man sitting in a large chair who smiled and beckoned to me. "Please sit down," he said with a broad smile. "I can't buy whatever it is you might be selling, but I welcome the sound of a voice."

That was the beginning of a friendship that lasted for almost twenty years. The man, Nelson Fortner,* was in his early fifties.

* Name has been changed

He had been employed in a bank, had managed to buy a small house, support a wife and two sons. Five years earlier he had been struck down with a stroke that left him paralyzed from the waist down. He could no longer work.

His medical expenses had been huge, making necessary a mortgage on the house. Mrs. Fortner obtained a job in a department store, and the two sons, who were in their final years of high school, found part-time work that brought in some additional money. Social Security was relatively new then, and many of the amendments that were eventually added were not yet in effect; therefore the help the family was able to obtain from federal or state agencies was small.

Mr. Fortner's condition had become stable. There was no hope for improvement. He had become only a shadow of the robust man whose photo he showed me. The family was busy earning money to meet the bills and keep the house running, but at noon Mrs. Fortner would hurry home to give him lunch. At night the boys would carry him to bed, and in the morning move him to the chair where he spent all his waking hours. Although his family loved him, they had come to think of him as something like a piece of furniture that had to be moved from time to time.

But he wasn't despondent. His positive outlook was amazing. He never gave up hope. "Sometime," he would say, and always with a smile, "sometime things will change. I know it. I feel it."

I liked Mr. Fortner and visited him as often as I could manage. His cheerfulness was like a tonic to me and made my affliction seem insignificant. During one of those visits I had an idea.

The telephone had been moved close to his chair so he could take messages for his busy family. My suggestion was that he make calls for me, beginning with the A's in the telephone directory, asking if there were children in the home, and explaining that I would photograph them and that there would be no charge if the pictures didn't please. For every appointment he made, I'd pay him one dollar, whether or not any pictures were sold.

He was eager to try, and from then on my business began to show a profit, for no longer was there a waste of time knocking on doors. Soon, because of his phone solicitations and word of mouth, I was able to open a small studio in the business section.

But then a problem arose. I was doing so much business at the studio that there was little time to go to homes to take care of the appointments made for me each day. But I knew how badly he needed the money, so I made the time to keep the appointments, going to the homes in the evenings and doing the darkroom work whenever I could manage.

Then one day I met a young doctor friend. While I had been in New York, he had become a physician. I wanted to stop and chat, but he was in a hurry. His wife was visiting an ill sister and his nurse-secretary was on vacation. He was worried that he might be missing calls from his patients.

Suddenly I had another idea. Why not devise some system by which a doctor could receive his messages when no one was at home or in the office? Telephone answering services, so familiar today, were unknown then. There were forty doctors listed in the telephone directory. I spoke with each of them and convinced fifteen of how beneficial the proposed service would be. The charge would be five dollars a month. I talked the idea over with Mr. Fortner, and as usual he was eager to try to make the plan work.

Fortunately it was only two months before a new telephone directory was to be ready. I saw to it that beneath the names of those fifteen doctors there was an additional listing: If no answer, they were to call Mr. Fortner's number.

The service was an immediate success. As each new directory was issued, more doctor's names included the answering service number. Also Mr. Fortner understood the possibilities and soon provided the service to electricians, plumbers, and many other businesses.

The effect on Mr. Fortner was dramatic. He became a businessman. A man of affairs. In four years he added so many new names to his list that Mrs. Fortner gave up her job to help with the book work and other details. A few years later he added a small room to the house. He called it "The Telephone Booth," and could enter and leave it easily with the wheelchair he'd purchased with some of his first profits. I had the first ride in a car he bought, modified so he could drive without the use of his legs.

My business prospered too, and although Mr. Fortner had long ago stopped making telephone solicitations for me, we considered ourselves partners in life; two handicapped people who had found strength in each other.

I don't remember when I began to notice that when our cars passed in the street, or met at stoplights or in parking areas, he always saluted me with a hand in which he held up three fingers. But he always made that gesture. When I visited him in his home there were so many things to talk about that I never got around to asking what that three-finger gesture signified.

After almost fifteen years of running his answering service, Mr. Fortner suffered a massive stroke. I was a frequent visitor at the hospital, and was always greeted with that familiar three-finger salute. During the final days, when he was conscious only part of the time, I made my last visit to him. And at last I asked him why he always greeted me with three fingers extended.

Mr. Fortner smiled and opened his eyes. "I thought you knew," he whispered, then slowly held up the three fingers. "The second one is you, Walter. The third one is me." His eyes opened wider as he put down all but the first finger.

"And surely you know Who that is." I could barely hear him. "We've been quite a trio."

I suddenly understood.

Why had I come back home? *Why* had I knocked on his particular door? *Why* had the ideas of the telephone solicitation and answering service come to me? We *had* been quite a trio. There *had* been a pattern. A picture completed.

Chance? Perhaps.

But I prefer not to believe that.

The Lines Between

BY BETTY TUCCINARDI
CHEMUNG, NEW YORK

*Mrs. Kaminsky was closer to us
than I realized.*

When I was eleven years old—many years ago—Mrs. Kaminsky was our neighbor in New York City. She lived across the alley from us, three floors up.

Since Mrs. Kaminsky carried some 300 pounds on a medium frame, her main activity consisted of "window watching," as she told my mother in a strong Yiddish accent. If people were on the street, she sat at the front window; otherwise she watched *us*, helping indirectly in the upbringing of my sister Patsy and me.

"Don't use your fingers—what will Mrs. Kaminsky think?" my mother would chide; or "Don't let Mrs. Kaminsky see you talking with your mouth full!"

Open windows in both apartments were an invitation for Mrs. Kaminsky to join our supper-table conversation. Once she warned me to move my glass of milk from the edge of the table so that I wouldn't knock it off with my elbow.

Often Mother would send Mrs. Kaminsky a plate of food via a pulley-line my father had rigged up between the two apartments, but she was always certain that she sent "clean" food to Mrs. Kaminsky, "because she's Jewish," Mother explained to me. Apparently "unclean" food was everything the Old Testament told Mrs. Kaminsky she couldn't eat.

On pleasant days, Mrs. Kaminsky painfully descended the stairs early in the morning on feet almost too small to carry her massive bulk. She would sit all day on two chairs placed together on the sidewalk next to the building. Mothers left their baby carriages within reach of her hand, so that when a baby cried, she would rock the carriage, while gently and smoothly droning. "Uhu-uhu-uhu-uh," her voice and a harder rock emphasizing the fourth note. Mrs. Kaminsky was a good "minder" of babies.

When her hands were free, Mrs. Kaminsky taught us girls how to knit and was an expert at picking up our dropped stitches. She also trained us in politeness. Woe to the child who passed her by without saying, "Good morning, Mrs. Kaminsky." That unfortunate one was immediately recalled into her presence.

"So what's the matter with your manners, hah? Don't you know how to say, 'Good morning, Mrs. Kaminsky'?"

Quarreling children were admonished. "How come you don't get along already? Don't you know God is watching yet?"

Mrs. Kaminsky became extra special to me the day I heard my sister complimented for her beautiful red hair and big blue eyes.

"No one ever tells me I'm beautiful," I muttered sulkily.

Mrs. Kaminsky put her heavy arm around me. "Betty, you have beautiful ways, and they shine through on your face."

Even though the mirror still revealed only a fat, round face and *straight* hair, I was mollified, and from that moment, Mrs. Kaminsky was my friend.

On Sunday mornings I would show her the pictures I brought home from the Presbyterian Sunday school and read the text to her. She would nod her head and murmur, "Just like the Jewish."

When I read the story of the birth of Jesus and explained that at Christmas we give gifts to each other because it is His birthday, she said, "I know. We give the children presents like that during Hanukkah."

"But it's not the same thing," I protested.

"Oh, yes. Both come from the heart."

As Hanukkah approached, I discussed with my mother what I could give to Mrs. Kaminsky. These were the Depression years, and there was little money for anything but necessities. My mother suggested that I offer to do some errands for her. "You know she can't go out."

When I told Mrs. Kaminsky about my Hanukkah present for her, she was very quiet for a moment. Then she pulled me onto her vast lap, "What a wonderful idea you have! So what I want you should do is to take a present every day to my grandson. He isn't old enough to come here and his mother is not so healthy."

On each of the next eight days, I carried Mrs. Kaminsky's present to her grandson, and each day, as I went back and forth between the two apartments after school, I grew more and more excited about the approach of my own favorite holiday. At last the twenty-fourth of December arrived. I was out on the street playing hopscotch when my mother lowered a basket with a package in it.

"Betty, take this box of cookies up to Mrs. Kaminsky. She wants to see you anyway."

All the way up the two flights of stairs, I breathed in the delicately sweet aroma of almonds so characteristic of Jewish homes at that time.

"Come in, darling," Mrs. Kaminsky called before I had a chance to knock on the door. My senses had not deceived me, for her daughter-in-law had made *schnecken*, which are raised sweet rolls baked on a bed of honey, butter, and almonds in an iron skillet. When they have browned, the skillet is quickly turned upside down to allow a rich syrup to caramelize on the top and sides of the *schnecken.* I needed no second invitation to reach for a bun and a cup of hot tea sweetened with a generous dollop of strawberry jam.

With the last of that goodness soothing my stomach, I guiltily remembered what I had come for and handed her the package with a "Merry Christmas." At the same time, she reached into the pocket of her shapeless dress and brought out a small box wrapped in white tissue paper and tied with a blue ribbon.

"This is for your Christmas," she said as she gave it to me. "You open it now and I open my own present."

Mrs. Kaminsky was already sampling the macaroon-topped cookies my mother always baked for the holidays, murmuring, "So good, so good," before I had the wrapping paper and ribbon smoothed for future use. I raised the lid and pushed aside the layer of cotton.

"Oh, beads," I exclaimed with delight. As I lifted up the pale blue beads, I was dismayed to discover that they were not the kind of beads I expected—they were a rosary, something for Roman Catholics, and I a Presbyterian. Whatever would I do with a rosary?

If Mrs. Kaminsky saw my momentary look of disappointment, she gave no sign. "My son took these to the synagogue, and had them blessed, and now I give them to you, my little friend, because I know they are for a Christian."

She put the rosary into my hand before going on. "Your Jesus is one of *us,* you know—a son of David!"

How was Mrs. Kaminsky to know about the rosary? Her knowledge of my Protestant faith was as vague as mine was of her Jewish religion, but as I thanked her—and meant it—I knew that that rosary, that string of meaningful beads, was drawing us together in faith as surely as the pulley between our two apartments had drawn us together in friendship.

Better Not Go, Oscar

BY OSCAR GREENE

There had been racial trouble in Boston,
and I was afraid.

It was lunchtime and I was at my desk, fumbling with a
newspaper. Suddenly, the paper slipped from my hands and
sprawled open to the death notices. My eyes focused on a
name: Ernie's family name. It was Ernie's mother who had
died, and the wake was to be that night. I looked more closely
and a chill ran through me. The wake was in a nearby city, and
that could mean trouble.

I laid the paper down and my thoughts raced backward. On
November 25, 1946, I was hired as a machine operator by a
large industrial plant located north of Boston, Massachusetts.
In early 1947, Ernie was hired. By chance, we met, shook
hands, and liked each other instantly.

On the surface we seemed to have little in common. Ernie
was sensitive, intense, quick-tempered and Italian. I concealed
my feelings. I was slow to anger, and I was black. Ernie lived in
a world of machines and he was a doer. I dreamed of being a
technical writer and I hated working on machines. Differences—yet our friendship grew.

Occasionally, after our three-to-eleven shift, Ernie would
insist I stop at his house where his wife Helen would have
homemade apple pie and steaming cups of coffee.

When strikes closed down our jobs, Ernie and I walked the
picket lines together. When Ernie's dad passed away, I rose early
and motored fifteen miles to attend the High Requiem Mass.

167

One day, Ernie approached, his face dark with worry. "Oscar," he blurted, "have the fellows been bothering you? Have they made any racial remarks?"

I was stunned, and Ernie hurried to explain. "Some fellows approached me," he faltered, "and they asked why we were so friendly. They said, 'How can you be friends with him, Ernie? Those people are all alike.'" Ernie's face reddened. "I told them it was none of their business who I was friendly with!"

I knew Ernie's temper, so I spoke quietly. "Ernie," I almost whispered, "you handled the situation nicely. Never argue with anyone on the race question. It's best to turn away quickly without a word. Remember, I have lived thirty-six years as a Negro and I'm an expert at spotting those who dislike me because I'm black. I've always felt those feelings were their problem and not mine." I paused for a moment and continued, "Ernie, I remember my football coach getting me aside and saying 'You're the only black player on the team, Oscar, and someone may dislike the idea. But always remember, they can't hurt you unless you fear them.'"

Time brings changes, and by 1957 Ernie and I were building apart. Except for infrequent telephone conversations, or a chance meeting on the street, we saw little of each other.

The months stretched into years, and by early 1975 trouble gripped Boston. United States District Judge W. Arthur Garrity ordered racial balance in the public schools to be achieved through busing. The cry "forced busing" pierced the air. To some, this was a genuine concern, to others it was a political stepping-stone. Some people turned ugly. Lone black men were assaulted by marauding bands of teenagers. In retaliation, lone white men were beaten if they chanced into some black neighborhoods.

This left me wary, and I avoided public transportation. Rarely did I leave home after dark.

My thought returned to the death of Ernie's mother, and I started the mental wrestling. *Why hadn't Ernie called? Should I attend the wake? I loved Ernie dearly, but we haven't seen each other for three years. Is it worth the risk?* People sometimes complimented me on the letters I wrote. Should I write him a letter, saying I had seen the notice too late to attend the wake? No, that would be dishonest, and there is no room in friendships for dishonesty. I would attend the wake and hope for the best.

At supper my appetite had shrunk to zero. My wife Ruby frowned and asked if I was ill. I looked up and said, "Ruby, Ernie's mother died and I'm attending the wake." She asked where and I told her. She gasped, "Oscar, you're not going over there are you?"

I responded with a confidence I did not feel. "Ruby, Ernie's my friend. This is the least I can do." She remained silent, but I knew she was afraid.

As I was leaving home, Ruby hugged me tight. "Don't be too proud to run," she said. And I knew it was more than teasing.

I got into my car for the fifteen mile drive to the funeral home. I started figuring out my battle plans. My thoughts raced. *Maybe I should remove my wallet and slide it under the seat. I had better drive into the funeral home parking lot and park as close to the entrance as possible. The less exposure the better.*

My hands were icy. It wasn't too late to turn back. A warm, caring letter still might do the trick.

The car purred on. By now I was hurling questions at myself. *Am I really being fair? If I'm severely beaten, who will provide for my family?* I drove on.

Within minutes the funeral home loomed in sight. To my horror, a hamburger stand had been built across the street from the funeral home and teenagers were everywhere. "That's it," I said to myself, "I'm going home!" But, something inside said, "Oscar, Ernie's your friend. If you're a coward this time, next time it will be easier to be one." I drove on.

There were no parking spaces near the funeral home's entrance. As I drove past, dusk was falling and the clusters of teenagers seemed to increase. In the middle of the fourth block a space appeared and I backed the car in. I eased out of the seat and headed for the funeral home.

Fear gripped me as I passed two groups of teenagers. They stopped and stared. I hurried on.

Within a block of the funeral home, someone darted from the shadows and fell in behind me. I hurried and the steps behind me quickened. A half block farther on, the person broke into a run and gained on me. Then, in a flash, he raced across the street and into the hamburger place. I almost fainted.

Seconds later I entered the funeral home, knowing that only half my journey had been accomplished. The home was packed, and I inched my way to the casket where I knelt and said a prayer. As I rose, Ernie approached. A sob escaped as he put his arms around me. Tears flowed down his cheeks. He struggled to control himself.

"Oscar," he said, "Helen told me to call you, but I couldn't. We haven't called each other for three years. How could I call and say my mother was dead?"

I tried to comfort him, but he broke in. "Oh, Oscar, I prayed you'd see the notice in the paper. I prayed you'd come!"

I hugged Ernie and left the funeral home. All at once I was no longer afraid. The bands of teenagers ceased to look like a mob; they were just youngsters enjoying themselves. Without knowing why, I remembered the words of my old football coach, ". . . they can't hurt you unless you fear them."

I walked quietly toward the car past groups of youngsters. At one corner they blocked the sidewalk. I circled and they parted. A boy smiled and said, "Good evening, sir." I smiled, too, and nodded.

I reached the car and eased into the seat. As the engine coughed, then hummed, I felt a marvelous sense of peace and thanksgiving. I had prayed to have the courage to show love and caring. Ernie had prayed that I might be there. Both our prayers had been answered.

The Old Fisherman

BY MARY BARTELS
PHOENIX, ARIZONA

I was tempted to turn him away.
He was so ugly.

O ur house was directly across the street from the clinic entrance of Johns Hopkins Hospital in Baltimore. We lived in the downstairs and rented the upstairs rooms to outpatients at the clinic.

One summer evening as I was fixing supper, there was a knock at the door. I opened it to see a truly awful looking old man.

"Why he's hardly taller than my eight-year-old," I thought as I stared at the stooped, shriveled body.

But the appalling thing was his face—lopsided from swelling, red and raw.

Yet his voice was pleasant as he said, "Good evening, I've come to see if you've a room for just one night. I came for a treatment this morning from the Eastern Shore and there's no bus till morning."

He told me he'd been hunting for a room since noon but with no success. "I guess it's my face. I know it looks terrible but my doctor says with a few more treatments . . ."

For a moment I hesitated but his next words convinced me, "I could sleep in this rocking chair on the porch. My bus leaves early in the morning."

I told him we would find him a bed, but to rest on the porch meanwhile. Then I went inside and finished getting supper.

173

When we were ready I asked the old man if he would join us.

"No, thank you. I have plenty," and he held up a brown paper bag.

When I had finished the dishes I went out on the porch to talk with him a few minutes. It didn't take long to see that this old man had an oversized heart crowded into that tiny body.

He told me that he fished for a living to support his daughter, her five children, and her husband who was hopelessly crippled from a back injury. He didn't tell it by way of complaint; every other sentence was prefaced with a thanks to God for a blessing. He was grateful that no pain accompanied his disease, which was apparently a form of skin cancer. He thanked God for giving him the strength to keep going.

At bedtime, we put a camp cot in the children's room for him. When I got up in the morning, the bed linens were neatly folded and the little old man was out on the porch. He refused breakfast but just before he left for his bus, haltingly as if asking a great favor, he said, "Could I please come back and stay the next time I have to have a treatment? I won't put you out a bit—I can sleep fine in a chair." He paused a moment and then added, "Your children made me feel at home. Grownups are bothered by my face, but children don't seem to mind."

I told him he was welcome to come again. And on his next trip he arrived a little after seven in the morning. As a gift, he brought us a big fish and a quart of the largest oysters I had ever seen. He said that he had shucked them that morning before he left so they would be nice and fresh. I knew his bus left at four A.M. and wondered what time he had to get up in order to do this.

In the years he came to stay overnight with us there was never a time that he did not bring us fish or oysters or vegetables from his garden.

Other times we received packages in the mail, always by special delivery: fish and oysters packed in a box of fresh young spinach or kale, every leaf carefully washed. Knowing that he must walk three miles to mail these and how little money he had, made the gifts doubly precious.

When I received these little remembrances, I often thought of a comment our next-door neighbor made after he left that first morning, "Did you keep that awful looking old man last night? I turned him away. You can lose roomers by putting up such people."

And maybe we did, once or twice. But oh! if only they could have known him, perhaps their illnesses would have been easier to bear. I know our family always will be grateful to have known him; from him we learned what it was to accept the bad without complaint and the good with gratitude to God.

Recently I was visiting a friend who has a greenhouse. As she showed me her flowers we came to the most beautiful one of all: a golden chrysanthemum bursting with blooms. But to my great surprise it was growing in an old, dented, rusty bucket. I thought to myself, if this were my plant I'd put it in the loveliest container I had. My friend changed my mind.

"I ran short of pots," she explained, "and knowing how beautiful this one would be, I thought it wouldn't mind starting in this old pail. It's just for a little while, till I can put it out in the garden."

She must have wondered why I laughed so delightedly, but I was imagining just such a scene in heaven. "Here's an especially beautiful one," God might have said when He came to the soul of the fisherman. "He won't mind starting in this small body."

But that's behind now, long ago, and in God's garden how tall this lovely soul must stand!

When God Speaks in Whispers

BY GENE L. MASSEY
ALTON, ILLINOIS

I love you, Pop."

"I love you too, John."

"I know."

"How do you know?"

"Because you've told me so more than a hundred times."

John is four, and I'm his grandpa. I'm not sure where the name "Pop" came from. He has called me this since he was able to talk. It was original with him. "We're buddies, aren't we, Pop?" he often says. And buddies we are.

I have always been aware of the influence an adult has on a child, and I'm especially sensitive to this with John. He always wants to put his red shirt on when I wear mine. He wants to wear his boots or his work hat when I do. "We're twins," he tells me, though sometimes it takes a lot of imagination on my part to see the resemblance.

John stayed overnight with me recently. He often does, and it's a special time for both of us. This particular time was extra special because it was the first time he had slept over since I had been living alone. John's grandmother—"Neeny" he called her, another of his original names—had died only a few weeks before, two days before Christmas, after a brief fight with cancer.

On this night, he and I did our usual things. Between baths

and bedtime, we popped corn, read stories, and played games. But this night we also talked about Neeny and all the things the three of us had done together. I could see that what we were doing for each other needed to be done. He was trying to comfort me. "I'll sleep next to you so you won't be lonesome," he said.

But I could see that John needed comforting too. The hustle and bustle of Christmas had denied us some of the necessary discussions which needed to take place at a time like this. John was feeling the hurt of his loss, and he also needed reassurance that he was still a very important part of my life.

John did keep me from being lonesome that night and what I saw when I awoke the next morning touched me in a way I shall never forget. It was one of those examples of a picture being worth a thousand words. Like bookends around my shoes on the floor beside the bed were John's little shoes, as close to mine as they could be placed.

"We're buddies, you know," John had said as we lay together before falling asleep.

People need people, especially when the moments are fragile, and the people are grandfather and grandson.

Look on the Heart

BY VICTOR W. WHEELER
WASHINGTON, D.C.

*Frank's face repelled me.
What could I do?*

He was the first customer to come through the door of my new lumberyard. But the moment he crossed the threshold, his strangely twisted, scarred face and fixed blue-eyed stare repelled me.

In his late twenties, he was slight of build and held his head low. He spoke in monosyllables throughout the transaction. I wanted his patronage but there was something about his ill-at-ease manner that aroused my suspicion: was he honest? Was he heavily in debt?

In checking his credit rating, I found that Frank Dandridge was a cement finisher and concrete contractor. There was no doubt about his qualifications; he had served his apprenticeship under one of the city's most highly respected general contractors. Nor was his financial reliability subject to question. Married, he had one child.

And yet, underneath it all, I didn't like his looks and hated to do business with him, much as I needed the money. My attitude distressed me so much that I prayed about it.

Then I remembered what the Lord had said to Samuel, "Look not on his countenance [or outward appearance] or on the height of his stature . . . for . . . the Lord looketh on the heart" (1 Samuel 16:7).

179

This passage really spoke to me. I simply would have to overcome my human feeling by asking God to help me with this relationship.

The frequency of Frank's trips to the lumberyard increased. Invariably he sought me out personally to serve him, but I could not look him straight in the face for fear of revealing my feelings toward him. It wasn't only his disfigured appearance but there was something furtive about the way he followed me about the warehouse. Sometimes I had the feeling that he was watching me; other times I could have sworn he wanted to talk to me on a personal basis but was hesitant to do so.

I continued to pray for him and for a change in my own attitude. I reminded myself that "there but for the grace of God, go I."

Weeks followed weeks and a gradual change in Frank began to take place. His conversation was more natural; he seemed less tense.

Yet I still had my original feelings of aversion and could not completely dispel my suspicions.

Then one morning Frank Dandridge came in to make a purchase. When his order was completed and put into his red pickup truck he scanned his load with more than usual thoroughness, suddenly turned on his heels and headed back into the office!

Naturally I guessed something was wrong, and his abrupt manner seemed to confirm my fears. As I followed him into the office, it flashed to my mind that the common brick I had in stock was not of the best color and hardness and that a few of the bags of cement were packed very hard, though it was all fresh merchandise. I bristled, ready to defend the quality of my merchandise.

Neither of us spoke for a long minute, as my customer

stared at me. A trace of a smile played on his lips, as at last he said, "You don't know who I am, do you?"

"Well," I haltingly replied, "I know you are Frank Dandridge, a cement contractor, and a good customer. Other than that, I'm afraid I don't know much about you."

There was another uncomfortable pause.

"I'm *Frankie.* Does that mean anything to you?" The young contractor stood expectant.

Frankie? I sifted through my memories but could find no answer. My consternation apparent, young Dandridge asked, "Do you remember a Mrs. Standish who once worked for you as a bookkeeper?"

"I do, indeed. But that was years ago."

"And do you remember her son and how he accidentally shot himself in the face while hunting?"

Of course, I remembered the little boy: an uncomplaining, courageous and, yes, handsome child—about eight years old. His father was dead and his mother had remarried.

"Well, then," Dandridge continued, "you must remember how you used to visit the boy after the accident and bring him toys and ice cream and draw funny animal pictures to make him laugh?"

My unattractive customer faced me motionless as sculptured granite. "That was eighteen years ago but I've never forgotten," he said.

A prickly sensation traveled up and down my spine. That small boy, bravely returning to school, stoically enduring the taunting of his thoughtless classmates about his artificial eye and scarred face, had not only stirred my sympathy but my admiration. I often had wondered what had become of the boy.

Frank Dandridge was obviously that boy. All manner of feelings swam around inside me.

"But, Frankie," I protested, "why didn't you tell me who you were that first day?"

"Well, from the moment I read the advertisement in the paper announcing the opening of your new business, I decided to be your first customer.

"I wanted to say 'thank you' in this way for the help you gave me so long ago," he continued. "I started to tell you who I was—I realized you wouldn't know the name Dandridge—but I thought you'd recognize me."

I felt ashamed. All the time I had been trying so hard to find the good in this man, to overcome my feelings of aversion, to see behind his unattractiveness, it had been his very goodness that had brought him into my lumberyard.

Suddenly from deep inside me came the words I had thought of the day I first met Frank Dandridge: *look on the heart.*

I looked at him now and for the first time I did not see scars. I saw his kindness, his desire to be friendly, and I recognized a brighter radiance in his personality.

I put my arm on his shoulder as we walked back to his truck. "Frankie," I said, "do you remember the day when you asked me to help you build a wren house to put up in the old cherry tree. . . ."

Because We Like You

BY DEBORAH H. LENZ
HONEY BROOK, PENNSYLVANIA

When we were first married, my husband and I lived on a street where there were many children. I longed to meet and know them, but they had no reason to come to our home, and my bout with polio as a child prevented my going outdoors to meet them casually.

But one spring day two young girls came knocking at the door. One held out a bunch of violets and asked:

"Would you like to buy these flowers for a nickel?"

"What would you do with the nickel?" I countered.

"Oh," she hesitated. "Prob'ly buy candy."

"Well, you see," I told her, "I'm not sure I should pay for flowers that God lets grow wild for us, but how about if I *give* you some candy just because I like you?"

That was fine, and I passed out some jelly beans.

Before they ate the first one, I knew I had at last made friends, for the spokesman, extending the bouquet, said, "And how about if we give you these flowers just because we like you?"

Love in Bloom

**BY CONNIE KELTON
DUMFRIES, VIRGINIA**

Friends are like flowers and should be treated and cared for with the same loving tenderness you would give your garden. First, make your selections and lay the groundwork carefully. Plant the seeds firmly so they will not wash away in an unexpected storm. Cultivate with kindness and understanding. Water frequently with thoughtfulness and consideration. Weed out all jealousies and misunderstandings. Do not fence in; this is the kind of garden which grows better when left free and open. Follow these directions and watch a budding relationship blossom into a full bouquet of friendship.

A Special Occasion

BY DRUE DUKE
SHEFFIELD, ALABAMA

When the doorbell rang that Tuesday morning, I was tempted to ignore it. I was up on the kitchen stool, straightening the top shelf of a cupboard and, running my house on a tight schedule, any interruption could disrupt my entire routine. But the continual ringing told me that the caller was not going to go away. So, grumbling aloud, I went to the door to find Mrs. Amy Rath beaming at me.

While Mrs. Rath is a nice elderly lady in our church, I could think of no reason why she should be calling on me. But there she was, a brown paper bag clutched in her hand, waiting to be admitted.

"Mrs. Rath," I began as she came through the door, "you've caught me looking a wreck."

"Forget it, my dear," she cut in. "You look fine. Anyhow, I didn't come to see how you look." She glanced at the sofa. "May I sit down?

"I get a little winded," she sighed, sinking down. "Here!" She held the bag out toward me. "I brought you something."

"How nice of you." I opened the bag enough to peek in—plums, great purple plums, piled one on top of the other. If there is one thing in this world I detest, it's plums.

"Goodie!" she was chirping. "I surprised you! No wonder. People are always surprised at how big and purple my plums are. You know"—she leaned forward as if she were sharing a great secret with me—"those plum trees were the joy of my

187

Joe's life. I believe he bought the house just because those trees were there." She sat back on the sofa, beaming.

Suddenly it hit me. She was giving me more than plums. These were her jewels, a part of her life she was sharing with me.

"Mrs. Rath," I said quickly, "what about a cup of coffee?"

"That would be nice, but please don't go to any bother." She followed me into my kitchen, chatting brightly about my curtains.

"We'll have to sit at the dining room table," I said. "My kitchen is such a mess."

"A special occasion!"

I glanced at her quizzically.

"A special occasion," she repeated. Then she chuckled. "Joe always called it a special occasion when we sat at the dining room table. We usually ate at the kitchen table, but when he came home and found the table set in the dining room, he said he knew it was a special occasion—like we'd gotten a letter from one of the children or maybe I'd made the checkbook balance." Her smile wavered a bit as though it might leave entirely. "Don't know when I've set my dining table," she said softly.

For the first time I really saw Amy Rath. She wasn't just the frail little lady in the second pew on Sunday mornings. She was a warm, living human, full of rich memories mixed with loneliness.

I brought out the remains of a lemon pie and we sat down to the dining table with our coffee cups.

"What special shall we call it?" she asked.

"Special?" Then I realized what she meant. "Oh, Mrs. Rath, your visit. That's what special."

And I meant it. The dancing eyes and cheerful voice of this

little old lady made me feel warm in a way I can't explain. Not once did I glance at the clock or even think of my schedule as she chatted gaily. The tales she told of her life with Joe and the children were threaded with golden strands of love shared in a time that I was too young to have known. I hated it when she said she had to go.

Holding her arm, I guided her out the back door. She turned her smiling face to me, and said, "I don't know when I've had so much fun. I hope I didn't talk too much. I know you were busy."

"I loved it," I declared honestly.

"Will you come to see me sometime?" she asked.

"I will," I promised, "on one condition. That we can have a cup of coffee at your dining room table."

"A special occasion! Oh yes, my dear, we can do that."

I kissed her wrinkled cheek and watched her go off down the sidewalk, head high, a lilt in her step.

After she was out of sight, I sat for a long time on the back stoop, feeling the warmth of the sunshine.

Suddenly I was crying. I knew what it all meant. God had so wonderfully shown me how He is often busy when I call on Him, how pitiful are my offerings to Him, how I many times need a Friend. Yet He is never too busy to listen. This had truly been a special day.

Part Seven

Unexpected Friends

The Friend
I Didn't Want
BY BARRY ALFONSO
SAN DIEGO, CALIFORNIA

I t was the first day of school and as I waited in the cafeteria lunch line, I looked across the room to see how many familiar faces I could spot. Then I saw a boy with large glasses sitting by himself toward the back, someone I didn't recognize. Curious, I asked a few friends who he was, but they hadn't seen him before either.

After lunch I asked the teacher monitoring the cafeteria about this new kid. She explained that he had just moved to this area and that it would be nice if I tried to make him feel welcome here. She added, a bit awkwardly, that he was mentally retarded.

For some reason I felt uncomfortable after asking her. Of course she was right—the kid, whose name was Matthew, was probably lonely and I felt sorry for him. But I didn't want to reach out to him either. It's hard to explain, but I couldn't see him as a real person. Being around him made me feel, well, strange. I felt guilty about it, too, and I tried to put him out of my mind.

I was glad that I didn't have classes with him. I saw him in the school hall everyday, going to or leaving the special class that he attended for students with learning handicaps. When I passed him I always noticed that he seemed happy and not at all like the lost, confused child I imagined he must be. He seemed at peace with himself—but I only saw him for a second each day and, anyway, how could I hope to understand a person like Matthew?

I had never spoken to him until the time he came up to me in the school library. I was doing homework when Matthew politely tapped me on the shoulder and asked me to read him something out of a magazine he was holding. He opened it to a page with a photo of a rocket launch on it; the article with it was on space travel and obviously too difficult for him. I couldn't refuse his request, but I didn't enjoy the experience. I was embarrassed. I didn't want any of my friends to see me with this retarded boy. *Why did he have to ask me to read to him?* I thought. I only half heard him thank me when I was through. I was glad to see him leave.

It didn't seem long after school had opened that Christmas vacation came. I had been looking forward to the holiday season for some time—and this year I had a special reason to do so. My Uncle Mark in Florida, a professional watercolor artist who specialized in seascapes, had hinted in his last letter that he might send me a gift. Since he knew how much I loved his work, it could only mean one of his latest paintings. For days I hung around the post office, watching the mails, awaiting that special package.

It finally came a few days before Christmas. I didn't open it, but the package's shape and weight told me that my uncle hadn't disappointed me. By the time I had finished some last-minute holiday shopping and caught a bus for home that evening I was debating whether to open it then or save my enjoyment until Christmas Day.

Just before I got off at my stop, I spotted Matthew sitting by a window in another part of the bus. I was going to say hello to him, to wish him a happy holiday. *But why bother,* I thought. *It won't mean anything to him.*

194

When I arrived home I put down my packages and then something struck me—my gift wasn't there! I was frantic. Did I leave it in a store? or on the bus? I called all the shops that I had visited that were still open, but they hadn't seen it. My leaving it on the bus seemed more and more likely. If that had happened, it was probably gone for good. I felt terrible.

The next morning as I was preparing to set out to search for the present the phone rang. It was a woman my mother knew calling, but she asked for me.

"There's a boy down at my house who says he's looking for you. Do you know him? His name's Matthew . . ."

I said I did. I was about to tell her that I had to be leaving when she told me something that made me almost drop the phone.

"Matthew has a package with him. He says it's yours. I'll drive him over if you'd like."

"Yes, that would be fine," I managed to murmur. I was still stunned when I put down the receiver. I realized that I had in fact left the present on the bus. I also realized I was thinking over other things, too—and they made me feel very ashamed.

There were so many things I wanted to tell Matthew when he arrived. I realized now that it wasn't Matthew who was lacking, but me. He wasn't the one to be pitied. I was, because of my narrow-mindedness. But when I showed him in and thanked him, the words just didn't come. I didn't need them anyway; I think he understood.

"You left this on the bus yesterday," he said. "I thought you wanted it." He explained how he had found it under my seat, then rode the bus again this morning to my stop and went looking for me on foot from there, asking anybody he met where I lived. His speech sounded so much clearer than the time he had spoken to me in the library—or maybe I was just listening better now.

I tried to pay him a reward but he wouldn't accept anything. He told me that his ride was waiting and he had to go. As he stepped outside, he turned and wished me a merry Christmas. I could only wish the same to him. I was too humbled to add anything else. As I closed the door my eyes were welling over.

I don't know where Matthew is today. His family moved out of town a few months after he returned the gift to me. But I know wherever he may be, he is still the same beautiful person. For what Matthew had inside—an honest, beautiful kind of love—could not be taught in a classroom, because it was born in him.

And he possesses a truth that he will share readily with anyone who will accept it—the truth of kindness. Matthew, the handicapped boy I once felt sorry for, taught me that even in the face of ignorance and misunderstanding, love can emerge. It's a rare and wonderful kind of knowledge.

The Miracle of Alma

BY DORIS HAINES*

I expected anger, I found a friend.

It was 1974, and the summer afternoon sparkled. I had driven this way a hundred times to and from my job at a cleaners, and yet, since my newly recovered health, I had the feeling that everything was brand-new. I looked at the green trees and lush grass surrounding the Los Angeles Museum of Arts. There was no traffic, even though it was already 3:15 in the afternoon. Only a few people wandered through the park. It was as peaceful as a Sunday afternoon.

I made a slow left turn on Sixth Street, my eyes lingering a moment on the park. Suddenly a woman's frightened face appeared directly in front of my windshield. For an instant I stared into wide blue eyes. Then she was gone, disappearing in front of my car. Automatically my foot slammed against the brake. The car stopped instantly. I sat frozen at the wheel, realizing that I had knocked a woman down!

Sitting stunned in my car, I heard the words "God, help me" coming from my throat. How strange those words sounded. I had never believed in God, yet here I was, calling on Him.

Overcoming my first shock, I ran to the front of my car, terrified at what I might see. And then I went limp with relief. A middle-aged woman, her white nurse's uniform smudged with grease, was slowly getting to her feet. Her purse had skidded away from her, scattering her few things about in the street.

*Name has been changed.

197

"Let me do that," I cried as she bent to pick them up. I gathered up her belongings, took her arm and urged her over to my car.

"Please sit down," I gasped, opening the car door.

Tears ran down my cheeks. I got in the car and pulled over to the curb. Trembling and crying, I looked at her. Fair-skinned, her pleasant face showed kindness.

"Just calm down, honey," she said. "God is with us and we're both okay, and that's what's important. You just relax a minute." Her voice was so gentle, and she reached over and patted my arm.

As she spoke, my cry to God for help came back to me. The first eight years of my life were spent in foster homes, before my Catholic grandmother and non-practicing Presbyterian grandfather finally found me and took me to live with them. But by that time I had already developed a deep sense of independence, coming from the need to survive during those difficult early years, and the confusing God-controversy between my grandparents convinced me that there was no God to depend on. There was only myself.

Believing this, for over thirty years I had used alcohol to face, or escape, reality until I realized it was destroying me. As a recovered alcoholic, I prided myself on the fact that even during those dreadful periods of uncontrollable drinking, I had never had an accident. And now . . .

"I'm going to call an ambulance," I cried. "We've got to be sure that you really are okay. And the police. I have to call the police." She put her hand on my arm.

"No, you're not," she said firmly. "You're not going to call anybody. I'm perfectly all right. In fact, I think I'm much better off than you are."

"But the car hit you! You *must* be hurt."

"You just grazed my leg with the bumper," she reassured me. "Of course it shocked me, and my knees just gave out. But I'm really quite all right."

Her sudden smile was warm. "My name is Alma," she said.

I tried to smile back. "At least let me drive you home," I said. "Though I still think I should call someone. You may be hurt without realizing it."

But she insisted that she was all right, so I drove her home and parked. I wrote out the name and telephone of my insurance company and gave her the paper.

"I don't want it." She tore up the paper. "I am not going to call your insurance company or anyone else. Don't you see, I don't want you to get into any trouble over this. It was an accident. There's been no harm done. I will not have you damaging your driving record. Goodness, you are suffering enough right now."

I stared at her. Why, only a few days earlier, in a supermarket, a woman had snapped, "Look where you're going!" when I accidentally bumped her shopping cart. Here I had knocked this woman down with my car and she was concerned, not about herself, but about me.

She told me about herself, of her Swedish background. At the moment she was caring for a lady in the LaBrea Towers who had only a short time to live. Her work was taking care of terminal cancer patients. She worked with those people only, because she was a nurse who wanted to make their days as easy for them as possible. She would not work in hospitals because the routine denied her the freedom of caring, of giving the love she felt she needed to give. She planned to stay with this lady until the end.

"Why do you do it?" I asked.

"Because they need someone," she said simply. "And

because God has given them to me. I feel He wants me to do this—to lead them to Him."

We exchanged telephone numbers. I told her I would call that evening to see how she was feeling. I went home and that night I said my first prayer in many years. I said, "Thanks." Then I said, "God, please let Alma be all right."

She called me later in the evening. "How do you feel?" she said, as though I were the one who had been hurt.

"Fine, Alma. How are you feeling?"

"My leg is a little bruised where the bumper hit it," she replied. "But it's nothing that can't easily be taken care of. I'm praying for you, dear. Have a quiet evening. Remember that God is with you."

"Do you really believe that?" I asked.

"I know it," Alma answered quietly.

I hung up the phone. I believed her. This feeling was something I had never known before. Never had I come in contact with another person who cared more for others than for herself. Here was a woman I had never met before, whom I had injured, yet who prayed for me.

Alma was serene. She seemed to have a special knowledge. The way she chose to live showed that she loved people. Love seemed to flow from her. It was a gift, and she was sharing it with me. For the first time since I can remember, I felt the presence of God. Hadn't He saved my life and given me good health? When alcoholism had me frightened and desperate, hadn't He shown me the way to a wonderful new life? And now, through the miracle of Alma, God had shown me that love is a way of life—His way.

We talked occasionally on the telephone after that. Finally, one day, Alma told me that her lady had passed away and she was going to visit her two grown children in San Diego.

I didn't hear from her again until I got a Christmas card that same year. She had taken on another case. This was her life. Her love was free-flowing. There would always be someone to receive it.

And—please God—someone to pass it on. An alcoholic man in my building came one day and asked to use my phone to call for help. Sick, mentally and physically, he felt he was going to die. We talked. I told him how I found sobriety, and how I found God. He listened. I was able to talk him into going to the hospital and surrendering to God's will. He did these things. Now, sober for over a year, we talk every once in a while. He tells me how grateful he is for my help, he prays to God every day for his sobriety, and he knows that he is loved.

Because of Alma, I now have a loving Friend whose presence is always with me. Sharing God with others, just as she shared Him with me, has given me the greatest inner peace I have ever known.

"Lisa, Are You My Friend?"

BY LISA KERR
JOHNS ISLAND, SOUTH CAROLINA
SENIOR, BISHOP ENGLAND HIGH SCHOOL,
CHARLESTON, SOUTH CAROLINA

I was fourteen and a pain in the neck, to be honest. I mean, I'd just run away from home; the best friend I'd ever had betrayed me in a way I never thought possible; my parents thought I was insane; and the only friends I had hung around me because, at the time, being a troublemaker's friend meant you were "cool."

The people I hung around ate up the stories I fed them of excitement and mischief. I suppose they respected me in some twisted way for having guts or something like that. But when I just wanted to be held or comforted, none of those "friends" were around.

The only person I felt deeply about, a boyfriend, I was no longer allowed to see. At first I prayed to God, "Please, please send me someone or something I can love again." Then after a while I stopped caring altogether. I had finally convinced myself and everyone around me that I had no need for anyone but myself.

I suppose that is when I became a *real* strain to deal with. And when my parents insisted that I had to spend the first two weeks of my summer working at a day camp for retarded kids, I acted mad. I wasn't really mad, just scared. Actually, I liked kids a lot. I told myself it could be worse. However, I didn't feel that way that very first day.

The volunteers and staff were required to ride the buses to keep order on the way to camp. I stepped up on the bus, smiled at the large black woman who was driving, and reluctantly headed toward a seat. There were about five kids on the bus already. I tried not to look at any of them too long, smiling weakly and blindly at each as I passed. They grinned shyly back.

"Sit across from me!"

I turned my head to see a large black girl sitting in a seat, holding a tiny blond-headed boy. "Right here," she said, slapping the seat across the aisle while balancing the small child dangerously on her other knee.

Almost afraid to say no, I sat where she told me, and before I knew it she was unloading her burden on me. "You hold Robby now," she said. "You work here, not me."

Looking down, I found myself staring into the large, vacant blue eyes of the little boy now in my lap. His mouth was open and wet, and his head bobbed up and down rhythmically as the bus bumped along the road.

"He can't talk," came the voice from across the aisle.

The black girl's eyes were still fixed on me. I was nervous but I tried to be kind.

"Oh," I said, "well, what's *your* name?"

"Karen," she beamed proudly. "I always hold Robby, but now you can. What's your name, girl?"

"Lisa."

"How old you, girl?"

"Fourteen."

"Ha!" she laughed loudly, pointing a kindly teasing finger at me. "You a baby. I'm seventeen!"

Seventeen! She acted like a three-year-old.

"Well, how old is Robby?"

"Six."

I was shocked. Robby was about the size of a two-year-old and he couldn't talk. He was a beautiful child, but he just kept babbling and rolling out sounds. His expression was blank; still, as the bus bounced and jolted along, he clung to me as if he knew I was there to protect him.

"You just wait till them crazies get on the bus," Karen was telling me. "Some of them really crazy." She tapped her temple with one finger, then moved it around in a circle.

I laughed. "Everybody's a little bit crazy."

"Hmph!" she said, throwing back her head. "You wait."

Robby was now standing and leaning toward the window. I slid over so he was right next to it. With his small hand he began spastically banging on the glass and calling, "Wawa." He was smiling. I looked out the window. We were crossing a bridge.

"Water," I said aloud. "I thought he couldn't talk," I told Karen.

She shrugged uncaringly. "He can a little."

"Robby, say Lisa," I said with slow deliberation. "Lisa." I pointed a finger to my chest. "Li-sa," I repeated.

For a moment he looked at me blankly, as if I were an idiot. Then he stretched forth a hand and put it on my chest. "Nana," he said.

I nodded happily. "Yeah. Lisa."

"Nana," he repeated, nodding his doll-baby head.

Karen broke into a childish round of laughter. "He called you Momma!"

"Nana," I corrected her, rolling my eyes.

As the bus began to fill up I grew apprehensive. Strange faces loomed at me from almost every seat. A few other volunteers and staff boarded and smiled, but none I took a particular interest in. Mostly there were children. Some of them asked me over and over again who I was. Others just swung shy faces my way from the front of the bus. I felt like an exhibit. Even the staff seemed to be checking me out.

I didn't care what any of them thought. I was only doing this because I had to, not to please any of them or to hang around these kids for two weeks. Did they really think I cared?

A pair of green eyes winked at me from the seat in front of mine. I stared back. All I could see was a round shaved head and the squinty eyes that kept watching me.

"Hi," I said to do something to break the discomforting stare.

A round, cherub like face with buck teeth and no chin popped up quickly and grinned at me.

"Hi," said the little man. "I'm Brad. I'm gonna marry you."

"What?"

"I'm gonna marry you," he repeated, grinning shyly. "You gonna be my wife, you gonna be my wife," he began saying in a singsong chant.

I rolled my eyes again. *Oh, God, why have You put me here? All these people are going to do is make me crazier. Why am I here?*

Brad followed me around the rest of the morning until the campers were divided into groups by age. I breathed a sigh of relief when I found I'd be working with kids from eight to twelve years old; Brad was twenty-six. I thanked God.

By the end of that day, though, I'd acquired more "followers." There was Charles, the freckle-faced kiss-o-holic who grabbed me and planted one on me every chance he got, and Daniel, a skinny, grinning little black boy who sweetly slipped his hand around my waist and asked me to be his "best girl."

And there was Jeni.

Jeni was a chubby, thirteen-year-old girl with short, curly brown hair, a pug nose, and large, liquid-chocolate eyes. She followed me around, continuously asking questions:

"Lisa, what did you have for breakfast?"

"Cereal, Jeni."

"Lisa, what's your middle name?"

"Katherine . . . Now hang on, Jeni, I'm doing something."

"Okay . . . Lisa, *what* are you doing?"

"Jeni!"

Her questions drove me out of my mind. All the kids did. I didn't want them to follow me or hug me or hold my hand. How could they be so presumptuous to think I wanted their attention? How could they expect me to care about them? I didn't even know them. I didn't want to. I was afraid to.

That night, I told my mom I wasn't going back. Of course, she told me I had no choice. So I went to my room and pouted, and once again told God, "This isn't doing me any good, God. I need something more. I need a friend. These kids depend on me to take care of them, but, God, I need someone to take care of *me*. Please help me."

No divine revelation came to me that night, so the next day I returned to camp, praying that the time might at least pass quickly.

On the bus, Robby was piled on my lap again, Brad sat beside me and Charles was waiting for me as I stepped off the bus. He placed a sloppy kiss on my mouth.

"Thanks a lot," I told him sarcastically.

He in turn flew into a hideous laughing fit and dashed madly across the playground to stalk another victim.

As soon as arts and crafts started, Jeni spotted me. I took a frustrated breath as she came and stood behind me.

"Hi, Lisa."

"Hi, Jeni," I tossed back at her half-heartedly.

"I missed you," she said.

I stopped what I was doing. Slowly I turned to Jeni, feeling an odd, almost warm sensation run through me. I faced her then. She was gazing at me with a tender, honest expression, waiting patiently for my answer.

"I—uh—thanks," I finally managed to spit out. I smiled at her with an unwanted feeling of gratitude. For what, I wasn't sure.

"Jeni," one of the staff members called, "come start your picture." Without another word to me, Jeni started off.

Before I even thought about what I was risking, I called, "Jeni, do you want to be my swimming buddy today?"

She turned, grinned a pleasant, beautiful grin, nodded and then kept walking.

Suddenly, Charles's kisses weren't so bad, and Brad's proposals were actually kind of flattering. Every day on the bus, Robby would reach for me and call "Nana." I would look at the little doll of a boy and wonder, *Why do you want me? What good am I? And why do I want you to need me?* All of a sudden I found myself looking at those children in a new, glorious light.

I had learned something very special about those children. They didn't have any standards that they expected me to live up to. Whether or not I was kind to them, they would always be kind to me. Their love was pure and innocent and unconditional. I had been so wrong to think them foolish for being so open with me before they even knew me! That was their gift, their wonderful gift from God. I was amazed and touched by the love they gave me. They would have loved me whether or not I ever learned to love them back. Perhaps their possession of, and my lack of, that gift would have made me resentful and jealous at one time, but somewhere along the line, those children had sparked something in me.

For the first time in so long, I looked forward to getting up in the morning. I now had somewhere important to go and important people to see. I went to camp with growing warmth every day. The kids loved me, needed me. They wanted me there. If I quit, they would be disappointed. I knew how disappointment felt. It was dark and ugly and cold. They had saved me; the least I could do was not let them down. I now knew why I was here.

One day my group sat in a circle and sang along to a tape of the song "That's What Friends Are For." Jeni was at my side, and halfway through the song she began whispering questions.

"Lisa, have you heard this song before?"

"Yes."

"Do you think it's pretty?"

I dropped my arm around her shoulder, and we swayed back and forth to the music.

"Yes, Jeni, I think it's beautiful."

"Lisa, are you my friend?"

"Of course I am."

"Lisa, do you love me?"

I wiped away a tear that fell on my cheek.

"Yes, Jeni, I think I do."

How to Be a Friend

Part Eight

The Big Noise Machine

BY FRANCES FOWLER ALLEN
SPRINGFIELD, ILLINOIS

*Tempers overheat when an air
conditioner comes between neighbors.*

In the early days of home air conditioners, we had the first
one on our block. My husband Bill was recovering from a
heart attack and had difficulty breathing in the summer
heat and humidity.

Our air conditioner was installed in the dining-room window, the most central spot in the house. "It's changed our
whole lives!" I marveled. "It's like having three months added
to the year when you *live*, not just endure."

The houses on our street were built close together. We were
separated only by a driveway's width from the house of an
elderly couple, the Sheltons. They were good neighbors. She
liked to garden and baked delicious goodies. He was retired
but kept busy at household repair jobs.

The third morning after the air conditioner's installation,
the doorbell rang early. I hardly recognized my kindly neighbor in the flushed, angry man who stood there.

"That . . . that *thing* is driving us crazy!" he snapped. "We
can't get a wink of sleep. You got no right to have that
noisemaker spoiling our peace and quiet!"

Dumbfounded, I tried to explain.

"You get that thing taken out," he demanded, turning away,
"or I'll go to City Hall."

"Forget it," said Bill. "They haven't a shred of law on their side."

213

I was shaking. "But it makes me feel awful! They're our neighbors!"

The minute Bill left for his office, I turned off the air conditioner. Then, toward noon, as the house started to heat up, I thought again about the air conditioner. "The Sheltons won't be trying to sleep now. I'll turn it on and have a cool house for Bill to come home to."

Later that afternoon I was emptying garbage when I saw Mrs. Shelton in her garden, weeding. "Hi!" I called. She turned away without answering.

This silent battle of nerves went on for days. Bill insisted on leaving the air conditioner on all night. The memories of waking up gasping for air haunted him.

One day when I returned home from marketing, I saw Mr. Shelton standing in our driveway glowering at the air conditioner. That night I poured it all out to Bill—my misery, their misery, how I missed their friendship. Bill was adamant.

The following night I was attending to some check-writing when I noted the envelope for a special offering the next Sunday at our church. I put in our donation. Then I turned to my Bible and began reading. Suddenly a passage spoke to me with a frightening appropriateness.

"So if you are about to offer your gift to God at the altar and there you remember that your brother has something against you, leave your gift there in front of the altar and go at once to make peace with your brother; then come back and offer your gift" (Matthew 5:23-24).

Just before I went to sleep that night, I prayed, "God there must be a way out. Will You show it to us?"

The next morning I had another talk with Bill. His attitude had softened. Finally he agreed to make another attempt to talk to the Sheltons and we went there together. Helen Shelton answered the doorbell. Her husband stood close by.

I stepped in, put my arms around her, kissed her cheek. "Oh, Helen," I said. "We've been such good friends. I can't bear this."

Meanwhile, Bill was muttering words along the same line to Mr. Shelton. "Sit down folks," Mr. Shelton mumbled.

Finally a timing compromise was worked out. We'd run the air conditioner until the Sheltons' bedtime, then shut it off till they had a chance to get to sleep.

Shortly after that, the heat wave broke and we had a week of rain and cool summer breezes—and didn't even have to run the air conditioner.

Toward the end of the summer, a smaller air conditioner came on the market and we bought one to put in our bedroom, which was on the opposite side of the house from the Sheltons.

"You know," Helen Shelton said to us one night, "I think one of those air conditioners might help Ned breathe easier at night."

I realized then how far we had come since those heated weeks of bitterness. "It would cool off the kitchen when I do my baking too," Helen continued. "By the way, you told me you were having company tonight. Could you use a plate of date cookies?"

So Much for Solitude

BY DON VIEWEG
WARWICK, RHODE ISLAND

*There was that same gaunt older woman
again, her arms wrapped tightly
around her thin body.*

I work in a high-pressure advertising job, so years ago I began
to spend my free time in lonely places where I didn't have
to meet people. It wasn't that I didn't like them; it's just that
I'd always been shy and I found that solitude helped me
unwind. That's why I liked jogging; it provided solitude, and it
helped me stay in shape too.

But one morning while I was jogging along West Shore
Road in Conimicut, Rhode Island, and enjoying the bracing
breeze of the Narragansett Bay shoreline, my attention was
drawn to someone I'd only vaguely been aware of on other
mornings. There was that same gaunt older woman again,
walking alone on the other side of the road.

Curiosity got the better of me. For the first time, I crossed
the road and found myself looking closely at her. She was
walking slowly, staring sullenly at the ground, her arms
wrapped tightly around her thin body as if holding herself
apart from the world. Deep, sad lines cut across her face. She
did not seem to notice me as I jogged by.

For days afterward I kept recalling that forlorn-looking
woman. How defeated she had looked! How very lonely! "She
looked as though she'd lost her last friend," I said to my wife,
Dorothy.

217

I found myself praying for the woman, wondering about her, wondering if I would ever actually meet her. Then, despite my penchant for solitude, I began to hope I *would* meet her.

But what will I do if I meet her, Lord? I prayed. Meeting people had always been hard for me. *I mean, wouldn't it be too forward to walk up and start talking to her?*

At once the thought came to me: *Smile at her.*

But no, I wanted to say, smiling just isn't natural for me. Ever since I was a teenager I've felt that my mouth isn't shaped right. My teeth aren't even and white. I've never liked my smile.

Smile, the thought came again.

Where had that thought come from? As a Christian I believe that God does speak to His children, but was that thought from Him?

Puzzled, I went into the bedroom and stood before the mirror, just as I'd done many times as a kid. I studied the face looking back at me. And just as I'd done back then, I decided to practice smiling.

It wasn't easy. I actually had to force myself. In the mirror, I saw the plaster of my face crack into a tentative, hopeful grin. With my cheek muscles I pulled that grin wider, feeling the jaw muscles tighten as I did so. It was more of a grimace than a smile.

I looked so ridiculous that I burst out laughing. But then I looked in the mirror again. At the tail end of the laugh—that was a *real smile!* When I wasn't trying so hard, the smile had occurred naturally!

Well, maybe I would try smiling after all, I thought.

But it was weeks before I encountered the gaunt woman again. There she was, her eyes staring straight ahead, her arms wrapped protectively about her chest.

I looked eagerly in her direction, gave her a good smile and . . .

Nothing.

I don't think she even noticed. Overhead a sea gull wheeled about, crying raucously.

My smile evaporated. I felt deflated.

But from somewhere deep within, a tiny voice seemed to prod me, saying, *Don't give up*. And I knew I mustn't. That woman seemed so lonely. It was important that she know *someone* cared.

The next time I encountered the woman was a few days later. She was still a block away when I spotted her walking toward me. It gave me time to work up an even better smile and to decide just what sort of greeting I would give.

She was still looking straight ahead as I approached. I found that smile and said cheerfully, "Good morning!"

Again, nothing.

Again and again over the following weeks the encounter was repeated.

"Hello!"

"Good morning!"

"Lovely day!"

The words were always mine. There was never a response. The only other sounds were the roaring of the surf and the pounding of my running shoes. Could anyone gain entrance to the woman's sad, silent world?

God, help me to reach her, I prayed that night.

"Good morning! Lovely day!" I shouted on our next encounter.

"Humpf!" she muttered, still staring stonily ahead.

But inside me, as I jogged on past, a kind of tension began to ease. *Praise God,* I thought. That "humpf" was like the opening of a door.

When I saw her again, she seemed different. Maybe it was my imagination, but it did seem to me that instead of her customary vacant stare, she actually recognized me. As I jogged closer, her arms were more relaxed and she was *staring* at me, her face puzzled.

"Good morning!" I shouted. "God bless you!"

She nodded. And there—ever so faintly—wasn't that a smile tugging at her lips? Yes! Yes, it was! I felt a sense of accomplishment as I jogged the remainder of my five miles that day.

The next time I saw her she was striding, head up, swinging her arms, looking boldly toward me.

"G-good morning," I choked.

"Morning," she replied softly, a timid smile on her lips.

Several days later we met again. This time her "Morning" was followed by a soft "Th-thank you!"

After that, the woman and I met frequently. I stopped to chat, first for a second or two, then longer. We had coffee, then several coffees. Her name was Pearl, and she needed someone to talk to.

Slowly, like the petals of a rose, she opened her life to me. Her husband had died ten years earlier. Her two married sons had moved across the country. Friends she had known had moved away too. She lived alone. And she confessed that she felt abandoned, hurt, angry, bitter.

"Until you started smiling at me, I thought no one in the world could ever care about me again," she said. "So I told myself I didn't care either. I didn't need anybody!"

After wiping her eyes, she continued, "But I learned from you what my wonderful husband had always tried to tell me: 'People really *are* nice, if you only give them a chance.'" Embarrassed, she looked down.

I took Pearl home and introduced her to Dorothy. They

became friends too. We took her to church, where she began to make more friends.

And now when I'm jogging along West Shore Road, Pearl often flags me down, saying, "I've been waiting for you! I have so much to tell you!"

Well, so much for solitude. But I don't mind. It's just as Scripture says: "Give and it shall be given unto you . . ." (Luke 6:38). I gave Pearl friendship, and in return God used her to give me something too—a new way of living. I'm more outgoing now and I like making friends.

All because of a smile.

How to Handle a Hassle

BY EUGENE LINCOLN
OLD HICKORY, TENNESSEE

Trouble began with a barking dog.
Unfortunately, it was ours.

The morning after Darlene, the children, and I had re-turned from a short vacation trip, a policeman knocked on our door. "Is your name Lincoln?" he asked.

"Yes," I answered. "What . . ."

"We have a complaint that you were gone for over a week without making any provisions for feeding or watering your dog. I'm giving you a warning citation."

I could feel my blood pressure rise. "Who made the complaint?"

"A Mrs. Carp* ," he said.

Of course! I should have known it! Even though we had not lived in this neighborhood long, we had been warned about this lady and her husband. Some children had told our kids that she was a witch, and her actions certainly seemed to merit the appellation. We had often heard her ordering children off the sidewalk in front of her house.

I started to explain to the policeman. "But we made ample provisions for our dog while we were gone. Our next-door neighbor fed him and saw that he had water. He had the run of the fenced-in back yard, and the garage door was left ajar so he could go in and out at will."

*Name has been changed.

223

"She also complained about his barking," the policeman continued. He must have sensed my feelings because he added, "This is only a warning citation."

I was furious as I told Darlene what had happened. I ended with, "Let's see those people later today and give them a piece of our minds!"

Darlene looked at me with the half-smile that she reserves for times when she is disappointed in me. "Would that be the Christian way to do it?" she asked.

"It's impossible to show brotherly love to folks like the Carps," I snapped.

"Well," she continued, "let's at least give it a try. We can just make it a friendly get-acquainted visit. Later we can apologize, then explain the provisions we made for our dog while we were gone."

"We won't get to the point of apologizing," I said glumly. "She'll run us off the property before that. Just you wait!"

Later my fears seemed to be proving true. At our knock Mrs. Carp looked out suspiciously, then opened the door ever so slightly. "What do you want?" she demanded harshly.

Smiling as if she were greeting her best friend, Darlene replied, "We're the Lincolns, Mrs. Carp. You know, we've lived here almost two months and we haven't paid you folks a friendly visit."

The door opened a little wider as Mrs. Carp said gruffly, "Come in, then."

In the simply furnished but neat front room, we noticed her husband, whom we had never seen before, half-sitting, half-lying, on a reclining chair.

"This is my husband," Mrs. Carp explained. "He has emphysema and doesn't talk much." Then, turning to him, she said, "Wilbur, these are our new neighbors, the Lincolns."

Darlene did most of the talking. If she hadn't, it would have been rather a silent time. She told them how happy we were to be in that neighborhood, about our children, and then about our dog, Muttso, and how he had frightened a burglar once.

"Our children really love him," she continued. "We're truly sorry if his barking has bothered you folks. We'll try our best to keep him more quiet."

The hard lines on Mrs. Carp's face grew a bit softer as she said, "Mr. Carp is quite nervous. He has asthma, too, and when he gets bothered by noise it seems to trigger an attack. Your dog did bark a lot."

Patiently Darlene described the arrangements we had made for Muttso's welfare. "We probably should have taken him with us," she said.

By the time we were ready to leave, Mrs. Carp actually smiled at us and invited us back. "You folks are the first visitors we've had in a long time," she said wistfully.

In the months that followed we paid the Carps several visits. As we got to know them and understand them better, we found respect and affection for them growing in our hearts.

One cold winter morning, as I shoveled drifted snow from our walk, an idea occurred to me. It was early Sunday, and I doubted if either of the Carps were up. I had almost shoveled the last bit of snow off their walk when the door opened.

"Wha—what are you doing?" Mrs. Carp asked in disbelief.

"Getting my morning exercise," I replied. "Hope you don't mind."

"Mind?" she repeated. "Why, it's the nicest thing you could have done for us. You folks are really good neighbors." She took out a hanky and dabbed at her eyes, explaining sheepishly, "This cold weather makes my eyes water."

I went home to breakfast whistling a tune under my breath. Darlene was right; the way of brotherly love *does* work. We had "got rid" of an enemy by making a friend of her.

Comforting a Bereaved Friend

Dr. Norman Vincent Peale

At one time or another each of us must give help to a bereaved friend. It is an enormous and sometimes very difficult task, but if handled properly, it can bring great comfort; if mishandled, it can make everyone very uncomfortable indeed.

Some time ago, when I was quite a young minister, I was visiting a woman who had just lost her husband. A Mr. Bayliss came to call. He walked into the living room with a measured shuffle, his head slightly bowed, his hat clutched in front of him. He sat on the sofa opposite me, and I noticed that he was perched on the very last edge of the cushion. I worried that he might fall off.

The bereaved woman was uncomfortable. She had been holding up very well until Mr. Bayliss arrived. Now it was she who had to make conversation.

"It's nice to see you, Mr. Bayliss. Robert used to enjoy so much working with you."

At the mention of Robert, Mr. Bayliss dropped his eyes and settled his mouth into a firm downward cast. After an uncomfortable twenty minutes Mr. Bayliss stood up. When he spoke, I'm sure he meant every word.

"Please, Charlotte. If there is anything I can do . . ."

Then he left, and the woman let out a sigh of relief.

I learned later that Mr. Bayliss had a wonderful sense of

loyalty and friendship for the bereaved. But, in the face of death, he somehow felt he had to put on an act.

Immediately after he left, the doorbell rang again. The new caller was another close friend, a Mrs. Aignell. I noticed that she paused in the doorway and closed her eyes for the briefest moment. I've often wondered if she used that moment for a flash prayer.

When she entered the room, Mrs. Aignell seemed at ease with herself, responsive to the mood of her grieving friend. They talked of the deceased naturally.

"I remember once," Mrs. Aignell said, "when Robert came to visit us . . ." And soon we were all exchanging memories of our friend. After what seemed a short visit, Mrs. Aignell stood up to leave.

"Don't fix supper tonight," she said. "I already have a casserole in the oven for you. I'll bring it over." When she came that evening, she unobtrusively left her Bible with several related passages thoughtfully book-marked.

Mrs. Aignell had discovered the art of helping a bereaved friend. Since then I have seen many people practice the art with great instinctive skill. I'd like to take a moment to mention some of the lessons they have taught me.

1. Let the bereaved friend set the mood. Reactions to death vary greatly. I have known people to lapse into a stunned silence; and I have known them to be somewhat hysterically laughing and seemingly jovial in their very grief; and I have known them to talk of suicide. Whatever a bereaved friend's mood, it is important to let him talk it out.

2. Do more than make the vague offer, "Let me know if there is anything I can do." You can always *find* something to do (and what you do is worth ten times what you say). Depending on how well you know the bereaved person, you might

attend to details around the house:—notify other friends, get supper, arrange for flowers, even make beds or wash dishes. Helping with these chores is important. One of the most touching comments on death that I have ever heard came from a young mother who had just lost her little boy. "Isn't it strange," she said. "I have to go on eating. But I don't feel like cooking anything if Bobby isn't here to eat it."

3. Be ready with words of solace if the right moment comes to speak them. One passage from John that Mrs. Aignell had marked is a favorite of mine: *I am the resurrection, and the life; he that believeth in me, though he were dead, yet shall he live* (John 11:25).

4. Try to find a way for your bereaved friend to help someone else. The great actress Helen Hayes lost her young daughter, Mary. It was only when Helen Hayes helped another mother, who had just passed through a similar tragedy, that she found real solace.

5. Remember it often takes weeks for the reality of death to strike home. Watch for this moment of climax and be ready to help again.

Sincerely...
BY SUE MONK KIDD

Today as I peer at the tiny crystals of ice on my kitchen window, I find myself thinking of my friend Mary. Diagnosed with cancer, she seems to have lost all hope. Her words to me were wintered and gray: "I don't want to give in to despair, but I have nothing inside to fight with."

A bitter wind gusts at the window, drawing my attention to the small green plant silhouetted against the pane. In spite of my preoccupation, I smile at it. This is no ordinary houseplant. This is my very own redwood tree.

I pour a bit of water into the bowl where it grows, remembering how I brought this little "experiment" home from my visit to Muir Woods, that magnificent grove of redwood trees along California's Pacific coast. Walking among the cool, misty trails of the forest, I'd arched my neck trying to take in their breathtaking size. The largest rose 253 feet into the sky, a monument of strength and durability. Touched with awe, I sat down on a bench nearby. How had this forest of ancient, towering trees survived the onslaughts of centuries? Fire, lightning, blight, earthquakes . . .

And then a park service guide ambled along the trail in my direction, and answered my questions. She mentioned how the bark was resistant to fire, decay, and insects. Then she pointed up to a large knotty lump several feet in diameter that was growing on the trunk of a tree. "Another secret lies in that burl," she said. "Hidden inside it are thousands of dormant buds. If the tree is traumatized, the burl is activated and sprouts new life. It's nature's way of insuring the redwood's continual re-creation."

Before leaving the forest I stopped to browse in the gift shop. That's where I came upon some tiny living burls for sale, complete with instructions on how to grow redwood sprouts. On impulse, I bought one and brought it home.

I placed the small piece of wood in a bowl of water and waited. Soon green bumps appeared on the burl, gradually unfurling into feathery shoots. Through the winter I watched it grow on my kitchen sill.

But now, suddenly, I look at it with the same sweep of awe I had in the redwood forest. I feel as if I am seeing one of God's loveliest truths spelled out. When life's traumas come—and they always do—there is tucked within us all a burl of buds, a hidden potential that enables us to fight back and grow again. For if God designed so beautiful a capacity in the redwood, how much more would he fashion within his children?

I gaze at the little redwood. I will take this burl to Mary, I think. Maybe it will whisper its truth to her as well: that in every crisis is an inner strength and hope just waiting to be tapped. Spring is on its way now. It can come again to the heart as well.

A Nice Trick

BY CORINNE UPDEGRAFF WELLS
FROM *TOGETHER*
METHODIST PUBLISHING HOUSE

Lured by a sign "Antiques," my husband and I stopped at a cottage where two elderly ladies ushered us into the living room and served us tea. When we asked to see the antiques, one announced hesitantly, "We're the antiques!"

"We needed friends," the other explained. "But how to make them? That's when we thought of the antiques sign. Only nice people appreciate lovely things. But remember, our sign doesn't say, 'Antiques for Sale.'"

"We've made so many lasting friendships," the other added, "that we know God isn't angry about our little trick!"

How To Be a Friend in Deed to a Friend in Need

BY BECKY COPPER
DUNWOODY, GEORGIA

Our time of greatest need began the week our older son Todd celebrated his second birthday. Shortly after I'd put our eight-month-old baby in his crib for a nap, I realized Todd was nowhere in the house! I ran frantically to check our backyard swimming pool. Todd was floating face down on top of the water. I pulled his limp body into my arms.

My husband Tom and I waited, praying, in the emergency room. "Todd's still alive," the doctor told us at last. "But there's been irreparable brain damage."

Todd was still in a coma when we finally brought him home. It took hours to feed and bathe him, to give him physical therapy. Needless to say, I didn't give much thought to matching up socks from the dryer, buying groceries, or taking our younger son for a stroll. But some of our friends did. One swept the walk, another cleaned the bathroom. Another brought a meal that could be heated whenever someone was hungry.

Three months after the accident, Todd wiggled his toe. Three months after that, he came out of the coma. But he'd developed cerebral palsy as a result—and years of struggle were yet to come. By then, however, Tom and I were able to look back and appreciate the help our friends had given us. Here's what we'd tell all those who *want* to help neighbors going through a crisis, but who don't know quite what to do.

1. *Let your actions do the talking.* As grateful as I was for verbal expressions of understanding and love, what I really needed was *help*—around the house, in making trips to the hospital. I finally put a sign on our front door for all the concerned neighbors who dropped by: "I'd love to have you come in—but please make yourself useful." It was wonderful the number who did, folding laundry, vacuuming, feeding the baby, while I attended to Todd.

2. *Be practical.* An outpouring of cards or flowers is nice. A bag of everyday items such as toothpaste, paper towels, and detergent is even nicer; it could be a big help to a family's strained budget. Don't send sweets. A pot of green beans is more welcome to someone who's been eating on the run.

If your friend needs a ride to the doctor twice a week and you can't spare all that time, find and organize seven more neighbors who can each drive once a month.

3. *Be positive.* A friend dropped by the hospital and said, "I'm taking you to lunch." Instead of lamenting the latest details of Todd's condition or recalling what a sweet child Todd *was,* she talked about the fun we'd had at our last get-together. I went back to Todd's room, smiling and relaxed, ready to reinvest my energies in his recovery. Staying upbeat was so important— especially around Todd, who might hear or comprehend— that I even put a sign on Todd's door: "Everything said in here must be *positive.*"

4. *Stand ready, but stand back.* I needed friends to support me—but not to push me emotionally into "understanding" or contact with others until I was ready. A woman with a brain-damaged daughter wrote me a short note: "I've been where you are, and I feel there will be times when I can help." Then she added her name and number. She didn't pressure me to

236

respond, but I gradually realized there *was* specific help—such as how to feed and communicate with Todd—that she could give me.

If a book, group, or other source of information or solace has helped you through a similar crisis, do share it. Just be sure it's pertinent enough to be of concrete help—and let friends use it as they wish.

Our crisis was a spiritual awakening for our family. As Todd slowly improved, we could look back and see how God's love had sustained us—a love made evident to us through our friends.

The Love Challenge

BY ANNAMAE CHENEY
ESCONDIDO, CALIFORNIA

One beautiful Sunday morning I was sitting in church, but I was not paying attention to the service. I was far too bound up in the trouble brewing at home with our daughter. Pam had been seeing a young man whom I had disliked from the very first moment I met him. He was a loser. But you couldn't tell that to Pam. That very morning we'd had another of our rows, one of those that ended with her saying, "I'm almost eighteen, Mother. I'll go with anyone I want," and with my shouting to a slamming door, "Until you're eighteen you'll do what I tell you!" *Oh, Lord,* I prayed—again—*give me some help with this problem.*

Now our new pastor's voice broke into my worried thoughts. "And so, today I give a Christian challenge." He was already in the middle of his sermon. "It's a challenge that few of you will want to accept . . ." It seemed as though he were looking right at me . . . "but those of you who have enough courage to take it on will find some rather surprising spiritual rewards. I challenge you to try making a friend of somebody you dislike."

At that precise moment Pam's boyfriend, Gene, flashed into my mind. *Somebody you dislike.* That was Gene all right. I could see him now with his rumpled clothes, his stringy hair and beard. I didn't like his sullen attitude, or the way he kept his head down, or how, when he talked, which wasn't often, he spoke so low that you could barely hear him. And how I hated that dirty fatigue hat which, indoors or out, he never took off.

239

The pastor finished his sermon. I stared into space. "I challenge you to try making a friend . . ." *Oh no, Lord, not him.*

"Yes, him."

I bowed my head and closed my eyes. *All right, Lord, I'll try.*

At lunch, I made my first attempt. It was a forced effort and it sounded false. "You've said that Gene was out of school," I said to Pam. "What does he do for a living?"

Pam was suspicious. And annoyed. I could tell she was trying to make up her mind about whether to answer. "I'm serious, dear. I'd really like to know."

"He doesn't have a job. He was working in a carpentry shop that folded. He's . . . looking."

That evening I told Bill how I'd accepted the challenge of making a friend of someone I disliked. He was surprised, and almost as surprised as I had been that I had chosen Gene. But Bill was interested immediately in what he called my "project." "How do you intend to begin?" he said.

"By asking him to do something for us," I told him. "Most people like to be needed. The roof needs fixing, and you haven't had time to do it. Couldn't we ask him to help?"

I waited until the next time Gene came to the house. Even then, I hesitated. I simply didn't like being around him, much less talking to him. But finally I took the plunge and told him about the work that we needed done. Would he be willing to give us a hand? The first thing he did was look at Pam. And Pam looked at me, perplexed.

"Sure," he said. It was little more than a mumble.

Bill took him up on the roof to show him what needed to be done. When Bill came down, he told me, "The fellow didn't say much, but I think he's going to be a good worker. He doesn't want any pay."

Bill was right. He did a good job on the roof, but it bothered me that he had done it for free. I didn't like the idea of being indebted to him. Besides, he needed money. I had just discovered that he was living out of his car.

A few evenings later when I came home from work, Pam and Gene were sitting on the front steps. With a swift prayer for guidance, I said, "Gene, you worked in a carpentry shop, didn't you?" He nodded.

"I have some antique oak furniture my father made about ninety years ago. It needs refinishing. Would you like to try working on it?"

He came into the house. He touched the surface of the old oak table, rubbing it with gentle fingers. The next day he stripped a couple of chairs and finished the wood on one, so I could see how it looked.

"It's beautiful, Gene. You're doing a nice job. Is there anything you can't do?" I asked.

"Yeah, I can't find a job." The bitterness in his voice startled me.

"You've got one now," I answered quietly. "There's a lot to be done here."

For the first time I could recall, he raised his head and looked directly into my eyes. I couldn't tell what the expression was that I saw in his. Gratitude, perhaps. Suspicion, more likely.

We soon realized Gene was the handyman the house had been needing for months. He painted, ran errands, repaired leaks, put down the kitchen floor and even worked on the cars. He was honest, hardworking, and seemed grateful for the money.

One night he and Pam came home very late. I was upset, and said, "Gene, I don't like Pam coming home so late."

"She's eighteen. She can do what she wants."

"Not while she lives at our house," I said angrily.

His eyes narrowed. "Maybe she'll move out then."

"That's her privilege, but if she does—she doesn't move back!"

We glared at each other. Finally, Gene looked away. Now I was worried. What had I precipitated? Had my spiritual "project" only thrown the two of them closer together? Maybe it was wrong to force oneself into an artificial "friendly" relationship the way I had done. A few minutes later, however, I overheard him say to Pam, "Your mom is upset when you're late. We'll have to get you in earlier."

From that night on, Gene changed. He whistled while he worked, looked up when he talked, and I soon noticed the ever present hat wasn't so low over his eyes. One day he mentioned his large family in the East whom he hadn't seen for a long time. His only brother was overseas in the service. He hadn't spoken with his mother in months.

"Why don't you call her?" Pam asked. Gene didn't want to. "Oh, Gene, you mustn't do that to her," Pam insisted. Her concern for Gene's mother touched me, and Gene, too, apparently, for later he did call home.

"Mom's sick," he told us the next day.

"Why don't we pray for her," my husband said, putting his arm lightly across Gene's shoulders. For a moment he stiffened, then he nodded.

Bill's prayer was brief—to the point: "Lord, we ask that You touch and heal Gene's mother, and give him peace about her."

The little prayer over, Gene walked quickly out of the house.

After that he telephoned home often, and one day he reported that his mother was feeling better than she had in a long time. Gene looked at my husband, "I've never known anyone who was in with God like you are."

"I'm not 'in' with God," Bill smiled. He's my Father, and yours, too. He cares."

"Maybe," Gene answered.

Gradually, it seemed to me, the bitterness began to leave him. And gradually I began to feel more at ease around him. Yet, there were things about him that continued to annoy me. That hat, for instance, the one he never took off. Finally I got the courage to ask Pam why he didn't have the good manners to take it off, "at least once."

"Didn't you know about that?" Pam said. "Last year three thugs jumped him. Almost killed him—ripped out most of his hair. He is *very* sensitive about it."

I felt embarrassed. For myself. For him. Could it be that Gene was not really sullen, just shy? Was it possible that a lifetime of hard knocks, and little, if any, kindness shown him, had produced his tough veneer?

Late one afternoon, Pam answered the phone's insistent ringing. She turned to Gene with a frightened look. "It's your sister calling. Your brother . . . overseas . . . Oh, Gene, he's dead!"

Gene took the phone, listened, then said, "I don't believe it—I can't!" His slender body shook with sobs as he hung up.

"What can we do to help?" I said, and I meant it, genuinely.

"I want to call Mom."

He took the phone in the other room, but returned in a few moments, and handed it to my husband. "She wants to talk to you."

"Don't let him be alone," his mother cried. "He loved his brother so much, he might do something to himself."

"He'll be all right. We'll keep him here with us." Bill reassured her.

Bill put down the phone. We were quiet for a moment. Then

Gene lifted his head and turned to Jim and me. "I wonder," he said, "if you folks would mind praying again." This time, though, Gene led the prayer. "Please, God," he said, "give Mom the strength to live through this."

When word came that his brother's body was coming home, I was the one who asked Gene if he wanted to go home for the funeral.

Tears came into his eyes as he nodded. "The whole family will be there."

"We'll take care of the airline ticket," I said.

He stared at me in disbelief.

"I mean it. Your mother needs you. You've got lots of sisters there, but you are her only son now."

He threw his arms around me. "You are the most fantastic people I have ever met!"

At the airport we watched Gene walk toward the gate. He turned, looked at us a moment, then, he took off his hat, waved it, and said, "God bless."

Tears stung my eyes. He had learned about God from us, and I had learned about loving from him. I'd learned about how wrong snap judgments can be, how vital it is to look at each human being as one of God's creations—just as I am one of His, too. And I'd learned that every one of us—strangers and friends alike—need each other's love. The pastor had been right after all, there were some "surprising spiritual rewards."

I turned to Pam as the plane took off. She saw my tears, and gave me a big hug. We had grown closer as a family in these last few weeks.

"You and Dad have been so good to Gene." Her voice broke, then she asked hesitantly, "Do you like him now, Mom?"

I answered with deep feeling, "I love him!"

244

The Gift of Friendship

BY TERRI CASTILLO
JACKSON HEIGHTS, NEW YORK

The subway car screeched to a halt and an unusually cheerful voice piped: "Eighty-second Street, Jackson Heights—and Merry Christmas, everyone!" Wrapping my scarf around my neck, I stared at the happy faces glowing under the bright subway lights. Women and children clung excitedly to colorfully wrapped boxes tied with shiny ribbons. Men chatted merrily, exchanging holiday greetings. The festive scene was unlike the usual somber subway rides. Tonight was Christmas Eve and the air was electric. For everyone, that is, but me.

This was my first Christmas in New York City. Leaving my family and friends back in Hawaii, I had moved here several months earlier—a young woman curious about the "Big City." It promised to be an exciting life, but it was sometimes a lonely one, and making friends wasn't easy. I'd hoped to spend the holidays with another young woman I had met in my apartment building, but she had been unexpectedly called home. Now, having no other friends nearby, I would spend Christmas alone.

As happy spirits escalated around me, I felt more and more homesick. "This is supposed to be a family celebration," I kept telling myself. "How can I celebrate Christmas without my family?" All I could think of was the empty room waiting for me, the television set my only company.

I slushed through the build-up of snow on the elevated

245

platform and trudged down the icy steps leading to the street below. Strings of twinkling lights crisscrossed overhead along the avenue, forming arches of stars against the dark night. From the little shops lining the street, the sounds of Christmas carols floated through the air. I tucked my head under the hood of my coat to block out the sights and sounds around me. They only made me more homesick.

Light flurries of snow swirled against me as I quickened my pace. I'd soon be home. Crossing the street, I saw the big church on the corner. It was aglow with lots of candles burning brightly inside. A life-size creche stood on the lawn with Joseph and Mary looking down at the Christ Child in the manger. A lighted sign next to it read "Please join us for Midnight Mass on Christmas Eve." A tear slipped down my cheek. Midnight Mass was a tradition our family never missed. We *always* went to church *together* on Christmas Eve. To go without them would only add to the pain I already felt. *Why,* I thought, *do I have to be six thousand miles from home this night?*

Inside the entrance way to my building I fumbled for my keys. Then I heard it. A soft, vaguely familiar voice singing: "Joy to the world, the Lord is come . . ." I stopped and looked around. No one was there. I listened curiously. ". . . Let earth receive her King. . . ." I poked my head out to the street. No one. I looked at the intercom unit on my right, and then I understood. The voice was coming from its speaker. Of course! In 6-B. She was a hearty soul who loved to stop residents in the lobby to chat—endlessly. More than once she'd told me more than I wanted to know about her herb garden and Felix, her house cat. Though she was a kind woman—she had brought me chicken soup one afternoon when she heard I had the flu—I had been avoiding her recently. I knew she was lonely, but I just didn't have the time to listen to her nonstop chatter. Now I could picture her sitting on the wooden stool next to the voice box in her kitchen, her wiry, silver hair tousled into a bun atop her head singing to the neighbors as they came home.

As I listened, my body lightened. Her voice rang out: ". . . Let ev'ry heart . . . prepare Him room. . . ." The words awakened me like a splash of cold water on my face. *Prepare Him room . . .*

Why this is what Christmas is about, I thought, *preparing room for Christ in my heart.* My mind raced back over the last few weeks. Had I prepared Him room? No, I hadn't. I had been too busy missing my family and friends. And in my loneliness I had *closed* my heart as tight as a clenched fist. To really celebrate Christmas meant I would have to *open* my heart—then I could make room for others. Maybe Christmas wouldn't have to be lonely after all . . .

Leaning against the intercom box, I drank in Mrs. Julia's radiant voice. "We wish you a Merry Christmas . . . we wish you a Merry Christmas . . ." she sang loudly. I pressed my finger on the button next to 6-B.

"Mrs. Julia," I said. "Mrs. Julia, this is Terri Castillo—down in 2-C."

"Merry Christmas, Terri!" she chimed back to me.

"Mrs. Julia," I said as a smile crossed my face, "how would you like to go to Midnight Mass with me tonight?"

The Friendship

BY PAUL SCOTT*

*It's been many years since this story of
a desperately afflicted and lonely young
man first appeared in Guideposts—
years that have given emphasis to the
haunting beauty of The Friendship*

At a time of utter despair, at a time when I could not go on, a remarkable man came into my life. He came with love.

I had run into disaster six long years before. A high-school senior, I loved dancing, good times, and sports. I was playing halfback on the football team when the first hint of trouble came. I couldn't seem to hold on to the ball. The condition grew worse. Finally I was hospitalized for extensive tests and at last my problem was diagnosed.

"You have leprosy, Paul," the doctor said.

Nowadays most doctors call it Hansen's disease. No matter what its name, to me it was a death sentence. My parents were horrified. Secretly, as if I were a criminal, I was whisked away to the Federal Public Health Service hospital in Carville, Louisiana, the only leprosarium in the U.S.

I was confined there for six fright-filled years—years of separation—lonely heartbreaking years.

Then medical science discovered new drugs—sulfone drugs—and they worked! But the new medication had arrived too late to prevent deformity. My life was saved, but my face

*Name has been changed.

249

was disfigured. I'd lost partial vision in one eye and I walked with a slight limp. My hands were severely crippled. Dr. Daniel Riordan performed sixteen operations in order to make them more efficient.

When at last I returned home, my parents could not accept my disabilities.

I was left utterly alone and could not cope with the hopelessness of my situation. Because of my face, I hated to go outdoors to the stares, the shock that followed my appearances. Old friends were uncomfortable with me. I would go out only at night, to walk the New York streets alone. One Halloween, my depression reached the lowest point in my life. Some youngsters, dressed in Halloween costumes and wearing grotesque masks, shrieked, "Look at him—he doesn't need a mask." At first they were joking, but as they looked, they realized it was absolutely true and they drew away.

I felt there was nothing to live for; there was no sense struggling. I was not a Catholic, but something impelled me to enter St. Patrick's Cathedral on Fifth Avenue that Halloween night. I don't know to this day if I prayed or not. I only remember that there—in the quiet of the huge vaulted cathedral—I began to think of Fulton Sheen. While I was at Carville, Bishop Sheen had visited there. I thought he would understand my feelings.

I saw a priest near the main altar and approached him, asking, "Could I please see Bishop Sheen? It's important."

The priest must have recognized, from my words or manner, the urgency of my request. He told me that the bishop was not associated with St. Patrick's, but that he would see that Bishop Sheen received my name and address.

To me, it was just another failure. Yet soon after that, I received a message inviting me to see the bishop in his office.

"I've come to you because I have no one else to turn to," I said. "I haven't a friend in the world."

"Well, now you have one," Bishop Sheen said, smiling. He invited me to dinner the next night. Soon after we began to eat, I had difficulty handling my knife and fork. Without stopping his conversation, my host reached over and cut my meat for me. That one very simple gesture touched me so deeply that I realized that I did, at last, have a friend. I poured out all the torment in my soul—my despair, my friendlessness, how I could not find a job, my lack of hope. . . .

"God has a purpose for your life, Paul," Bishop Sheen told me. "It is up to us to find it." In the weekly dinners that followed as the bishop invited me again and again, I found new hope.

"You won't have many friends," he would tell me. "But those you have will be real ones."

And so it has been. I'm grateful for the friends who have given me so much, and for the two dedicated physicians, Theodore Capeci and Carl Barlow, who provided, free of charge, several operations that greatly improved my appearance. My hands are still deformed, but they are much better than before the operations. Finding work was difficult, but I finally located an office job at a minimum salary.

I am so grateful for the gifts God has sent me. These gifts that have enabled me to persevere were there all the time, but it was through Bishop Sheen that I learned to recognize them. It was he who gave—not as a bishop but as a human being concerned about another human being.

What were those gifts?

I received the gift of faith. I have been able to accept Christ. The bishop himself baptized me in St. Patrick's Cathedral and confirmed me in his private chapel.

Each day I live is different from the next. Every day is not necessarily good; at times I still am overwhelmed with loneliness. But my faith helps me. I don't wake up in the morning and say to myself, "Today I'll have faith." Faith and belief are with me all the time and I don't have to consciously dwell on it. They're there—just as God is—and I can live in that assurance day by day.

I received the gift of love, spiritually and materially. My friend helped furnish my apartment, provided clothes and once, between paydays, when he discovered I had no food, insisted on taking me to a delicatessen where we filled a shopping basket for me.

I received the gift of acceptance. Although filled with resentment at the things that had happened to me, I learned to accept myself, to be less bitter and to work on what I can offer to others—good manners, cleanliness, neatness, respectability, a sense of humor.

I received the gift of security, of knowing that any time I am too lonely, too depressed, I can reach Bishop Sheen. "If you can't get me by phone, send me a telegram," he told me. Now that he lives in Rochester, New York, I miss him greatly. Still, I have learned now to rely more upon myself. I have learned the security of faith.

Last year Bishop Sheen included me in the guest list for his installation as Bishop of the Diocese of Rochester. I was sitting at the end of a center pew and had a good view as he proceeded down the red-carpeted aisle of the cathedral after the ceremony. There were many well-known people present, but, suddenly, he stopped by me. He put his arms about my shoulders saying, "It's nice to have you here, Paul."

I said something in reply and became conscious of an increased murmur all about me, of necks craning. The lady sitting next to me must have wondered, as others probably did, who I was. She whispered, "Are you a representative from the Vatican?"

Her question amused me. "No," I answered. "Just a friend."

The lady looked at me for a moment and then softly said, "He must love you very much."

She had used the one perfect word—love.

Editor's note: *Paul Scott's faith continues to sustain him. He is now unable to work because of his physical condition, but he is a volunteer at a social-service agency that helps troubled people with their problems. Archbishop Sheen encourages Paul to have this interest in others—"to reach out and see that you can be helpful despite any limitations you have." Paul has given well over 1000 hours of volunteer service.*

Archbishop Sheen, who retired as Bishop of Rochester in 1968, is now Titular Archbishop of Newport, Wales, and devotes his efforts to writing, lecturing (mainly at secular institutions) and conducting retreats for priests, sisters and laity throughout the world.

Hansen's disease (leprosy) can be cured, but it must be diagnosed and treatment started early, before crippling and deformity begin. Patients can be treated at home; they do not have to be isolated from the community. To learn more about the disease, its detection and treatment, write: *American Leprosy Missions, Inc., 297 Park Avenue South, N.Y., N.Y. 10010.*

The Pickle Disaster

BY JEANETTE PARR
DECATUR, ARKANSAS

Making friends the hard way.

For two months we'd lived in the leafy, red-clayed community nestled close to a sheltering Arkansas mountainside.

I had thought it would be like coming home again—after all, I'd been reared on a small farm—but even on this bright Saturday morning I found I was homesick for our previous life in suburbia. I put in a long-distance call to my best friend Anna. For a little while I merrily described the scenic beauty and stalwart, land-loving residents, but Anna saw through my disguise.

"Have you told anyone how lonely you are?" she asked.

I stared at the phone and imagined her straightforward gaze boring into mine. "Oh, Anna, I've wanted to. But you know how hard it is for me to share my feelings with people I don't know very well. I always start tap dancing around those feelings."

She chuckled. "I know. But I'll bet there's a lot of folks there who believe in bearing one another's burdens—including yours. You've got to make that first step."

I promised to try. After we said our good-byes, I glanced out the window of the sun-splashed, high-ceilinged kitchen at our two small daughters, busily placing globs of rust-colored mud into their toy stove. Then I looked inward, at myself as a young girl—a tall, chunky, klutzy one. I remembered what it was like growing up on the farm, a place where everybody else seemed to be practical and efficient. The women could cook and sew and can, and the men could not only farm but repair everything from pocket watches to tractors, and I, the "bookworm" and impractical daydreamer, had felt inadequate. I'd tried to compensate by developing a quick wit and perfecting an ever-ready smile.

I hadn't thought about my younger self in years, but Anna's comment about my loneliness was true. Here in this brambled, foreign place, away from my close circle of friends and our life in faster-paced suburbia, the old feelings of awkwardness and uncertainty had returned. I'd been hiding behind a stack of one-liners ever since we'd arrived. People here now saw me as Miss Totally Cheerful. What would they think if I suddenly stepped off stage and admitted the truth, that I was really Mrs. Down-in-the-dumps, Mrs. Hungry-for-Friends?

I untangled my infant son from the phone cord and swung him to my hip. Burying my face into his soft curls I whispered to God, "Father, give me the courage to develop some honest relationships here."

"Yoo hoo!" A knock on the back screen door interrupted my lonely prayer. I recognized the voice of Mrs. Stockton, my "next-door-neighbor" who lived a quarter of a mile away. Her stout figure, round sunbaked face and merry black eyes reminded me of the gingerbread people I baked for the children. Today, a large straw hat was crammed over her curly gray hair.

"I brought you something, dear!"

I looked down at a tattered basket overflowing with plump green cucumbers, placed next to a large ceramic crock and a box full of dust-coated glass jars.

"You liked my pickles so much at the church supper, I figured you'd want to make some. So I brought the lime, new lids and rings, the jars, pickling spices *and* my famous recipe! All you have to provide is the sugar."

I looked at her beaming face. "Uh, that's really nice of you, Mrs. Stockton. Won't you come in for a moment?"

She took off her hat and fanned as she refused, telling me she'd been up since sunup making pickles. Now she was rushing home to can string beans, and then she'd help her husband Leonard in the chicken houses. "The heat is getting to the chickens," she told me, "and I've got to bake some rhubarb pies for tomorrow night's fellowship supper at the church."

Just listening to her schedule, I began to feel tired.

As her jeep roared away I began lugging in her gifts. Irritable thoughts accompanied every move I made. Why hadn't I told her I didn't know how to make pickles? Glancing at her recipe, I saw she had listed "a pinch" of this and "a dash" of that. If I'd asked, surely she would have interpreted for me. More importantly, why hadn't I told her I had other plans for today?

I stared at the basket of cucumbers. They'd have to wait until Monday. Or could they? I didn't know. And I was too embarrassed to call anyone and ask. Now anger pushed all guilt aside. She'd had no right to bring those stupid cucumbers without asking first!

Still, I couldn't let them spoil. My whole family had loved the lime pickles. So, after checking a cookbook and finding no recipe, I reread Mrs. Stockton's "famous" recipe. I'll just take a guess at the pinches and the dashes, I decided as I dumped a load of the green offenders into the sink and began washing them.

That evening, before going to bed, I looked in on a crock full of lime pickles sitting on the shiny, flower-sprigged linoleum. They were supposed to soak in the lime solution twenty-four hours; I would put them in jars on Monday.

When the Stocktons' hoarse roosters signaled the birth of a new Sunday, I awoke to a strange-smelling house. Quickly donning my old robe, I followed my nose to the kitchen.

"Oh no!" I shouted so loudly that my husband rushed out from the bathroom; his half-shaven jaw dropped several degrees when he saw what I saw. The kitchen floor was covered with a greenish-gray foam. A thick river of popping bubbles was still foaming over the rim of the crock. The sticky mass could have captured starring role in a science fiction thriller.

I heard a quiet chuckle. "Those pickles will never make it to the county fair."

No, my mind yowled, *and neither will I!*

Outwardly, I remained calm. "You're right about that. Go back to your shaving. I'll clean up this mess."

I tracked through the foam, grabbed the mop and a dented metal bucket. Then I filled the bucket with water and began attacking the goo. By the time I had captured and annihilated it, the time had come for our big-family-one-bathroom Sunday morning scramble. In spite of heroic efforts, I arrived at the gray-shingled church smelling faintly of lime.

That evening, the fellowship hall was alive with activity as we entered. Clumps of teens were bunched around the antique piano. The long-haired pianist was pressing out a tinny rendition of "Do Lord" on the chipped ivory keys. Chubby-legged children were whizzing around everyone's knees and weathered men were gathered around the back doorway swapping tales. Flushed-faced women were flitting back and forth between the kitchen and the groaning tables.

As I began removing our food from a large picnic basket, Mrs. Stockton appeared at my elbow. "How did the pickles turn out, dear?"

"They . . . really pickled!" I just couldn't tell her we'd dumped them in the tall weeds behind the smoke house.

She gave me a pleased look and began placing spoons in the vegetables. One slipped from her hand and clattered on the worn tile floor. She stooped to retrieve it, then straightened, a flustered look on her plump face.

"Uh, dear, I have something to tell you, and I hope you won't take offense, but it's always best to be honest about things, you know." Her voice had that special pitch one uses with tiny children and fragile old people.

Surely she hadn't guessed about the pickles! With a guilty flush, I met her gaze.

"Your shoes don't match," she said.

I looked down at my feet upon which I'd slipped one red and one navy blue shoe. I looked up into Mrs. Stockton's compassionate eyes.

"You can just slip out that side door and no one will ever be the wiser." I knew she meant that, but suddenly I began laughing.

"No, Mrs. Stockton, I'm staying right here. You're right. It is best to be honest about things; now I have something to tell you!"

I told her about the pickles, and we both began laughing hysterically. A crowd of curious onlookers began to gather around us.

"Since we're being so honest, I have something else to tell you," Mrs. Stockton gasped. "I gave you those cucumbers because we had such a bumper crop and I was so sick of putting up those pickles that I told Leonard if I had to put up one more I'd scream!"

That confession brought on another gale of laughter. Now we had the undivided attention of everyone in the room.

259

"Let us in on the joke," someone urged.

I looked at the ring of expectant faces and my heart began slamming against my ribs. *Give me the courage to develop some honest relationships.* My own prayer was gently returned to my consciousness.

Now here I was, standing in the presence of most of the community with a chance to share my true feelings. I could "tap dance" in my red and blue shoes—and make a big joke out of this whole incident—or I could use this opportunity to walk into honesty. I'd never felt more vulnerable. Or more sure of the right choice. God had opened the door. I had to talk—to share—to trust my way through it. Even if I stumbled in the process.

I pointed to my feet. "I wore mismatched shoes tonight." Gentle laughter rippled around me. "And I've *felt* just like they *look* ever since we moved here."

I told them how lonely I'd been and how out of place I'd felt, even though I'd pretended everything was just fine.

Mrs. Stockton squeezed me in a bear hug. "Why, honey, that's just the way I felt when Leonard and I moved to this jumping-off place. I was considered a newcomer for years, but now I'm as good a hillbilly as these born-and-bred ones."

More laughter. Then hugs. And the fellowship supper that followed was truly that—a time of fellowship—as others shared the times they'd felt ill at ease and frightened in new situations. I thought of Anna's comment about finding people who believed in "bearing one another's burdens." And joys, I might have added.

I'd found people like that here, and I knew that no matter where I lived I'd always find them. In God's wonderfully varied, extended family. Because I'd conduct an honest search.

Part Nine

Seeing Beyond

The "Artist" and the Waitress

BY KATHIE KANIA
THE DALLES, OREGON

Mustard!" my mother exclaimed, looking up from the TV show we were watching. "Mr. Bishop*asked for mustard on his hamburger and I never took it to him!" There was a look of unsalvageable regret on her face. Honestly, the President of the United States didn't take his job any more seriously than my mother did waiting on tables at Meeder's Dairy Bar, a popular eating place on the maple-lined Main Street of Ripley, New York.

"Oh, Mom," I mumbled without looking up. "It's no crime to forget. Mr. Bishop would have asked again if he'd wanted mustard that bad." I could speak with authority because I was waitressing too, in nearby Erie, Pennsylvania, but my job was just a stepping-stone until I could get something I'd be proud of, something in the art world.

I was grimly grateful that this interim job kept me and my apartment afloat, but inwardly I disliked it. I worked dependably, with clenched teeth, all week long, and then retreated to my parents' farm near Ripley on my day off. I felt tired in body and mind, and I didn't like to be even *reminded* of work. The nails-on-chalkboard voice of tipsy old Harold still rang in my ears: "Where's my dinner? It's gonna be cold by the time you get it here."

*Names of customers have been changed.

263

Every Friday evening he staggered in, always ordered the same dinner and always with some caustic comment. I had been admonished by the staff to "bear with poor old Harold," but it was hard—especially on the Fridays that the cook ran out of his favorite side dish, cottage cheese with chives. That brought more surly remarks. And this Friday there'd also been the big fat guy chewing a wet cigar as he made a great display of a wad of money in his wallet. No, I didn't like to be reminded of work.

Mother, on the other hand, was tickled that we were in the same "profession."

"How do you abbreviate french fries on your orders?" she asked, smiling. "FF?"

"Oh, Mom, *I don't know* . . ."

"C'mon. You know. Is it FF? I use FF. Some waitresses write 'fries.' I don't think it's necessary, do you? Writing 'fries'?"

"Oh, Mom." You'd have thought we were famous painters discussing techniques at some big important gallery. Someday I would be famous. Someday I would excitedly discuss my work. But not now.

Later, on this evening off, Mom and I went to the local basketball game. How good it was to be back at the big brick high school—to cheer as the lights gleamed on the gym floor, to wash away the grimy memories of the week! The large gym resonated with cheers, clapping and the drumming and squeaking of basketball shoes as we took our places on the bleachers, and then the crowd roared "Go, Ripley!" as the teams rumbled by.

"Number nineteen!" Mom shouted at me over the din. "See him? He and his girlfriend were in Meeder's last night!"

"Fish dinner every Friday, he and his wife," Mom yelled to me, making sure I saw it was the Ripley coach.

While the game went on, I couldn't help laughing as the players and audience became pointed-out individuals who "always ask for relish" and "love coconut cream pie." How odd it seemed: I had come to the game to forget my job, and Mom had come to look for her customers.

Late that evening at home I asked her, "How do you do it, Mom? I mean, how do you maintain such a good outlook with your customers?"

"Well, first of all," she said, "they're not customers—they're people, just like you and me. All I'm trying to do is make things as nice for them as I can." It was a kind of paraphrase of the Golden Rule that I'd heard from her many times before. "The joy just seems to come back around to you," she concluded.

That talk made an impression on me, and after that, my week seemed to go a little better. I began to relax my martyrly attitude and to look a little differently at the people I waited on. By the following Friday I even felt ready for Harold, who bumbled in on schedule. I forced a smile and said, "Harold, I'm glad to tell you that we have cottage cheese with chives today." I peered into his eyes hoping for some bit of friendliness, but there wasn't much there.

"Then bring me my usual, and don't take all night about it," he snarled.

A few nights later I stepped tiredly from the Greyhound bus in Ripley and walked over to Meeder's, where Mom would be getting off soon. I sat looking into my coffee as she bustled by the counter to tempt me to indulge in pie or to pat my collar and say her ancient "Every mother crow thinks her baby is the shiniest."

"A healthy crow never complains without caws," I reminded her absently. But I didn't feel much like joking.

A high school football player lumbered in and sat at the counter.

"Oh, hello, Bob, what can I get for you?" Mom asked him.

"Let's see . . . fries and a burger, I guess. And a Coke." Mom wrote the order down, then hesitated with a concerned look.

"Now, Bob, that's a lot of *fried* food. Have you had any vegetables today?" I wanted to pull my coat over my head and crawl under the counter. I thought of Harold. What in the world would this guy say to this intrusion?

"Well, no . . ."

"Wouldn't a nice little salad taste good with this?" she smiled down at him.

"Sure," he smiled pinkly. "French dressing, please."

That night Mom and I sat on the couch going through a box of old pictures. "The difference," I announced flatly as I shuffled a small pile of photos into a neat stack, "is that the people in Ripley are *nicer* than the people in Erie. You don't have to deal with some of the people I do."

"Oh, I don't know . . ." Mom said mildly. "I guess we get our share." She thought a moment. "The Warren brothers give me a hard time. They call me 'old slowpoke' or 'turtle,' then they laugh and try to get others to laugh."

"Oh, Mom, don't you just hate it? Doesn't it make you want to just scream?"

"Well, it does make a person feel bad . . ."

"Do you ever say anything back to those creeps?"

"No. Remember the Bible verse 'Love your enemies . . . If you love only those who love you, how does that make you any different from the heathen?' [from Matthew 5:44-47]. No, I just sort of go along and ignore it."

"Mom, what's this picture?" I had come to an impressive black-and-white of three young women posed by a typewriter

266

in a large, sumptuous office. A warm smile illuminated Mom's face as she took the photo from me.

"Oh, yes! This was taken when I was a private secretary at the Texas Company in Houston. Those were some ladies I worked with. We thought we were quite spiffy," she said, nodding toward the fashionable clothes and suave '40s hair styles.

I looked from the stylish young woman in the picture to the one before me dressed in her blue polyester uniform which still held a faint odor of FF's. Mom was better educated than I. She'd begun the career of her choice. And when, after years of marriage and children, she chose to return to work, she took the available waitress job uncomplainingly. Instead of filling her workdays with a lot of regret and one eye on the want ads for something better, she threw her whole heart into the job at hand. "Whatever your hand finds to do," she used to say to me, "do it with all your might" (Ecclesiastes 9:10). That was Mom.

In the months that followed I can't say that old Harold changed a bit. But I did. And so did the job. It became an adventure.

One day an elderly lady asked me, "Are you part owner here? You seem to really care about the customers."

"Well, actually, I'm an artist," I told her. "But right now I'm a waitress." I might have added that every day, I was using my artist's eyes to see each customer as a person!

Pals

BY PATRICIA BRADY

*One was a blue-eyed towhead, the other
was brown-eyed and dark, but they were a
lot alike—even in their need for healing.*

Although the McCurdy family lives around the corner
from us, my son Jackie didn't really get to know Danny
McCurdy until they started school. I guess it was my
fault. Even though I truly like people, it's difficult for me to be
the one who reaches out first. I'm always afraid I'll seem a little
foolish.

Once Jackie and Danny did get acquainted, though, it
became apparent to me that the bond of love between them
was something special. I'd never seen anything like it in the
friendships of my three older children. And I wasn't the only
one who thought the boys' closeness rare. As the two little pals
became a familiar sight in our neighborhood, more than one
neighbor commented, "I never see those boys argue." And it
was true. Whatever activity one suggested, the other agreed to.

Because of their physical appearances, it was easy to spot
them at play. Jackie's blue eyes and blond hair contrasted
sharply with Danny's brown eyes and straight dark hair. Unfortunately, there was a greater—though invisible—contrast between them. Jackie's excellent health was marred only by
eczema on his legs, but Danny had lost a kidney to cancer
before he started kindergarten.

When the boys turned seven, Danny's cancer recurred. This
time part of his right lung was removed, and chemotherapy

treatments were started. The treatments made Danny violently ill, and whenever I heard he was having a bad day, I had only to look at Jackie to confirm it. Jackie, who visited Danny whenever possible, would get so uptight he couldn't sit still, and he would scratch at his eczema more than ever.

Soon the chemotherapy caused all of Danny's hair to fall out. He tried to conceal his head by covering it with a red Phillies baseball cap. Whether Danny was sitting in class or at our supper table, the bright red cap clung to his head.

At first, I didn't realize why Jackie was badgering me for a cap exactly like Danny's. But as soon as he got it, Jackie placed the cap on his head the same way Danny wore it—with the brim turned toward the back. And, like Danny's, Jackie's cap stayed firmly in place from sunup to sundown. No amount of persuasion could convince him to take it off.

That July there was a special healing service at our parish church, and I had a growing feeling that Danny should attend it. There were to be several priests on hand to anoint the sick with oil. I asked Lorraine McCurdy, Danny's mother, if my husband Jack and I could take Danny. She agreed to let him go.

When the evening of the mass arrived, Jack and I took our children and Danny to the church. It was hot and crowded inside. Perspiration began to darken the rims of the two red baseball caps and trickle down the boys' faces, but neither removed his cap.

Finally it was time for those seeking healing to go to the altar. "How about it, Danny?" I asked. "Do you want to go up and ask the Lord for a healing?"

"Nah," Danny said, his lashless brown eyes avoiding those of the people rising from their seats. "I'm sick and tired of being prayed over."

I knew, of course, that it was actually a case of "sick and tired of being stared at," something Danny had come to dread. Even though I understood that feeling only too well, I was upset by his answer. If anybody in that church needed a healing, it was Danny.

"What are we going to do?" I whispered frantically to Jack.

"I've got an idea that might work," Jack answered softly. Turning to Jackie, he said, "What about you, Jackie? Would you like to have prayers for your rash?"

I don't know what went through Jackie's mind as he pondered his father's question, but I know what raced through mine. *Do it for Danny, Jackie,* I pleaded silently. *Do it for Danny.*

"Okay," Jackie decided. "I'll get my rash prayed over."

My husband and I stood up and started to move forward. Our son slid from his seat and headed for the end of one of the lines. Danny, tugging at his cap, followed at his heels.

When we finally inched our way to the altar, we found that we'd been waiting in Father Curran's line. He was our parish priest and knew the boys' needs even better than they themselves did.

"Well, Jackie," he said. "What healing do you want from the Lord?"

"I want to get rid of this itchy rash, Father," he said, pointing to his bare legs. Then Father Curran looked at Danny and his gaze softened. "And what about you, Danny? What do you want?"

Danny grinned shyly. "I'm not here for me, Father. I'm here for Jackie's rash."

Father Curran anointed the boys with oil and, placing a hand on each, began to pray. Jack and I, who were standing behind them, also laid our hands upon the children and prayed along with Father Curran. Jackie's rash practically forgotten, we silently begged God for Danny's life.

A few days later I was sitting on the beach at the lake, watching the two red caps bobbing about in the water. Jenny, a friend from church, joined me.

"Pat," she said joyously. "Danny's been healed."

My heart leaped. "How do you know?"

"I had a vision of Danny dashing into the lake and you know what? He wasn't wearing his baseball cap. His hair had grown back in thick, black curls."

I wanted desperately to share Jenny's confidence, but something was wrong with that vision. Danny's hair had been straight. Yet soon after that, Lorraine McCurdy told me she could see hair starting to appear on Danny's scalp. And when it was finally in, we could all see for ourselves that it was thick—and curly.

When Danny returned to the hospital for his checkup, the doctors informed the McCurdys that Danny had responded to treatment. The cancer was arrested. The rejoicing in the Lord that took place in our parish was indescribable. In fact, my own gratitude to God was so overwhelming that weeks passed before I realized Jackie wasn't scratching at his eczema.

"Come here, Jackie," I said the afternoon it finally occurred to me. "Let me see your legs." He rolled up his jeans. The skin on his legs was clear.

Four years have passed since the night of the healing service. Danny and Jackie, now eleven, are as close as ever and—except that Danny's hair has returned to its naturally straight state—are pretty much the same as the summer they were healed.

As if those of us who witnessed this miracle from God weren't blessed enough, He has heaped upon us His grace to overflowing. For no matter what the future holds for Danny and Jackie, the Lord has spoken to all of us through the love of two small boys. Hasn't he shown us firsthand how to become like children so that we, too, may enter the kingdom of heaven?

As for me, I got a healing of my own. Now, whenever I find myself in a situation where I feel a little foolish reaching out, all I have to do is think back to the night of the healing mass and that desperately ill little boy who did not hesitate to step forward—no matter how "foolish" he may have felt—to help his friend.

Can I do less?

A Favor for Anne

BY OLLIE A. TROLINGER
SAN BERNARDINO, CALIFORNIA

*There was something she wanted
done—after she was gone.*

It was a Sunday morning in May with the scent of honey-suckle sweet in the air, but I saw none of the beauty. I was boxed in with my own personal troubles in my small world. The great depression was at its worst. As I dressed for church I asked myself, "Why bother to go?"

It would just be another humiliating experience. Everybody knew that my husband and I had been forced to move in with my parents because we could not support ourselves. My husband's long unemployment had aggravated a chronic illness so that he was unable to work even when jobs were available.

"Hurry up," my mother called up the stairs. I opened my mouth to tell her I wasn't going to church, then decided that she'd be hurt. I'd go today, but before next Sunday I'd tell her I couldn't face it anymore.

As soon as the service ended, I hurried outside to wait for mother alone. And as I waited, my friend Anne Lawson came toward me. The sunlight filtering through the branches of a giant maple tree sent ripples of gold through her hair.

"I've been wanting to see you," she said. "I'm sure you've heard that the doctors say I have only a few months to live. Whatever I'm going to do, I must do now."

"Yes," I said, "I've heard and I'm so sorry." There was so very much more I wanted to say but I couldn't.

Coming closer and dropping her voice, she said, "There's something I want you to do for me—after I'm gone. Will you?" she asked urgently. "Promise me you will!"

"Of course," I answered. "You know I will! What is it?"

"I've told my children I want them to look to you as an example. When I was younger, facing the same problems you're facing now, I gave up too easily. I didn't fight. I want my children to grow up to be fine and courageous, like you— never compromising, never giving in."

"Oh, Anne," I pleaded, "I'm not a good example!"

Her eyes looked into mine. "All I ask is that you let them know you. Let them see how you face life's challenges."

I walked home at mother's side, stunned at this estimate of myself. If only Anne knew what a weakling I was! If she knew how close to quitting I'd felt that very morning! Well, I'd have to stop all this self-pity. I couldn't give up now, not with Anne's children watching me. How insignificant my small problems seemed when I looked at hers!

By the time the burnished leaves on the maple had fallen, Anne was gone. A pall of gray dust hung over Missouri; farmers left their homes; it seemed that everyone was out of work. My husband's illness was worse and I still had found no teaching job. There were many applicants for every position, and kick-backs were common. Upon making application for a job in a country school, I was told that a Miss Kellogg had offered to split her first month's salary among the trustees. What was *my* offer?

I thought of Anne's children, almost daily visitors in our house now—thought of sharing this day's activities with them. "Nothing," I answered. "If you want a teacher who will pay elected officials for a job, then you don't want me!"

That night there was a loud pounding on the door. My

husband opened it to find the same trustee whom I had seen earlier that day. "Here," said the man, thrusting a paper into my husband's hand. "Give this contract to your wife. Tell her we want her kind of influence on the children in our school."

Many times during the next few years, I found myself pulled up short, thinking, when a question of ethics arose: "I can't do that; it wouldn't look right to Anne's children."

And meanwhile I watched Anne's husband, a wonderful father, bring up a fine family. I often reflected guiltily how little I had really done to justify Anne's tremendous compliment. A bit of advice, a word of encouragement—actually they seemed to need little of either.

Gradually my husband's health improved; during the post-World War II boom his construction business flourished. Our days of poverty were almost forgotten. Anne's children now had children of their own. My husband and I moved to California, and I hadn't thought about all this for years until last summer a friend and I were reminiscing about old times.

As we talked, I saw myself again—young, worried, and at the crossroads. Suddenly Anne Lawson stood before me, in front of the church, just as she had long ago, her hair glowing golden in the speckled light. I found myself relating this story to my friend. And as I told it, I heard it myself for the first time.

Anne, Anne, that fine brave example I was to set—that was not for your children's sake. It was for mine.

Secrets in a Summer Sky

BY JEAN HAGER
PAWNEE, OKLAHOMA

*Was it true that if you looked real hard,
you could peek through the stars
into heaven?*

It is raining, and when it rains, I remember Fleety.

I was nine that summer and first saw her while sitting on our front stoop watching the new family next door unload their furniture from a pickup truck.

Fleety was in the back of the truck, between the stove and refrigerator. Then she leaped deftly over the side, sauntered to the edge of the yard and stood, spraddle-legged, staring at me. She was ten, skinny, all knees and elbows, and there wasn't a spot on her anywhere big enough to put a finger on without touching a freckle.

After a while I began to squirm under the silent probing of Fleety's hazel eyes. So I went inside to report on the new neighbors' furniture to my mother. My mother said that I must be very kind to Fleety because she had heard that the child wasn't well.

Fleety soon was the acknowledged leader in our block. We only had to say, "What can we do now?" and wait for Fleety to think of something. And she always did.

One time Fleety thought of making capes from old sheets to see if we could fly. After we had the capes tied around our

279

necks and were about to climb up the rose trellis to our garage roof, Fleety suddenly clutched at her throat and sat down on the grass.

"What's wrong, Fleety?" I asked.

Her face had suddenly gone as white, freckles and all, as the piece of sheet tied around her neck.

"I guess the sun is too hot," Fleety said in a matter-of-fact voice. "Maybe I'll just go inside for a little while." She smiled at me, but her eyes had that funny look they got sometimes, as if she were far away. When she came outside later that day, she looked and acted the same as always. But she didn't mention flying again.

The best times of all that summer were the evenings after dinner when Fleety's mother would spread quilts on the grass in their back yard. I would go over and lie beside Fleety and her mother and father on the quilts and look up at the stars.

I remember one evening in particular. Fleety's mother brought out a cardboard fan, the kind they had in church, with funeral home advertising on it. She sat beside Fleety and fanned the hot air over Fleety and me.

That was the night when Fleety said, "The stars are God's windows. If you look real hard, you can see into heaven." I squinted my eyes and looked hard at one large star, but I couldn't make it out. Fleety could, though. "The streets are solid gold and there is never any night there, nor sickness, nor crying," she said.

Later, when we saw a falling star, Fleety said that was how you could tell that someone had died, and that it was God's elevator coming down to meet the departed. Fleety's mother stopped fanning then and went into the house.

Right after that, Fleety stopped coming out to play. Her mother said she was sick and had to stay in bed. One day I was walking around my yard, bored, wishing Fleety would hurry and get well and come out to play again. My glance fell on a few late roses growing along the back fence. I picked some, wrapped a wet newspaper around the stems and knocked on Fleety's front door.

Her mother came. Her eyes seemed sunk into her head. She moved woodenly to accept the bouquet and was about to go back into the dark house when she turned suddenly and asked if I would like to see Fleety.

The house was silent and shadowy because all the blinds were down. Fleety was lying on a worn couch. But she was no longer the Fleety I had known. She seemed hardly more than a shadow. Her eyes were closed; but as I stood staring down at her, she opened them and for a moment there was a familiar spark.

"Don't cry for me," she whispered. "God's elevator's coming."

Then she closed her eyes, and I stumbled out to lean against the rotting porch railing. For a few moments I could not see at all. And then slowly it came to me. Some indomitable something in Fleety could never die. It was years later before I could put a name to that something, or the "image of God."

I can't recall that it rained very much that summer, yet it's always the rain that reminds me of Fleety. Sometimes at night when I am sitting in my room, reading, the rain against the windowpane sounds like fingers tapping. And when I look out into the wall of night swirling and pushing like a river against the glass, I see Fleety's thin face and I feel her presence.

Since these few years we have on earth are but a brief moment in the scheme of things, I know that someday I will discover what it's like where Fleety's gone—how it feels to be inside God's windows, looking out.

A Long, Cold Walk

BY HARVEY BROWN
CHICAGO, ILLINOIS
AS TOLD TO RICHARD H. SCHNEIDER

*At last there was a job opening,
but it was seven miles away and he had
no money for carfare.*

One thing I have learned in my thirty-six years: When it seems things can't get any worse, they can. But I also discovered something else one cold day seven years ago: There's nothing so bad that some good can't come out of it.

One day in January 1982 my wife, Emmie, and I were standing on an empty elevated platform on Chicago's north side waiting for a train. I had been out of work for some time, and pretty discouraged; nobody seemed to want to hire a 350-pound man with a visual handicap. In fact, I am legally blind. So is Emmie. We had just cashed our Social Security disability checks, a total of $630. We planned to use all the money to pay our rent and bills.

A bitter wind off Lake Michigan whipped down the platform, and Emmie snuggled close to me. Suddenly she squeezed my arm. "Somebody's here."

Squinting out of my right eye, which still has enough sight so I can make out shapes, I saw them: two men with guns.

"Let them take what they want, Emmie," I said. "Our lives are more important."

After the robbers ran away, Emmie and I trudged back to

our apartment on North Winthrop Avenue, where we reported the robbery to the police. Then we collapsed in despair. The men had taken almost every penny we had.

We eked it out for a few days, but I knew we'd never make it if I didn't find a job. Before the robbery I'd just about decided to give up; nothing ever seemed to work out. Now I knew I had to try.

I could do some things such as maintenance work, and with a powerful magnifying glass I could read. One evening we found an ad in the *Chicago Tribune* classifieds for a maintenance job at the YMCA at West Chicago Avenue and North Dearborn Street, just north of the Loop downtown. Applicants could show up at 9:00 A.M.

"Tomorrow morning I'm going down to get that job," I said.

"Why are you so sure you'll get it?" asked Emmie.

"'Cause I'm going to be the first man there."

"But you don't have any money for carfare." The bus was a dollar.

"Honey," I said, "Harvey Brown is going to walk."

"Oh, Harvey . . ."

I knew what she was thinking. I was overweight and could barely see, and Chicago and Dearborn was nearly seven miles away. But I figured I could make it in two hours of steady walking.

Come dawn Monday, though, it didn't look so good. The weatherman said it would be the coldest day of the year—the wind chill factor making it even worse. "Better bundle up," he advised.

"Harvey, you'll freeze," cried Emmie. "Don't go."

"Honey," I said, "if you don't go, you don't *get*." I didn't usually talk that way, but now we were desperate.

I pulled on two pairs of long underwear, two pairs of jeans, three shirts, four pairs of socks, and three coats. I kissed Emmie good-bye, walked down the stairs and out into a cold, gray Chicago. It was 6:45 A.M.

As I turned the building corner, the wind screamed at me like a wild animal. I hunched down into my coat and, with hands shoved deep into pockets, pushed down Thorndale Avenue to Broadway.

I navigated by using shapes of distant buildings as landmarks. I don't watch for traffic, but I listen for it. An occasional car hissed by, and my footsteps were the only ones I heard. My nostrils froze each time I inhaled, so I was careful to take little breaths.

Old windblown newspapers scrabbled at my ankles as I turned left on Broadway heading south. By the time I had gone about a mile my toes were getting cold. But the eastern sky over the building was lightening a little and I was glad it wasn't snowing. *Too cold to snow, I guess.*

Suddenly my foot flew out from under me, and I grabbed at the icy metal of a newsstand. Panting clouds of steam, I realized I had to be more careful; frozen patches of snow were like greased iron.

I continued down Broadway, squinting into the windows of warm-looking stores. A display of living-room furniture looked so nice. When I got this job, maybe we could put some money down on a sofa.

After about an hour I reached Clark and Diversey; I couldn't feel my toes any longer. I stepped back as a big CTA bus rumbled by, the stench of its hot exhaust filling the air. I turned down Clark heading toward Chicago Avenue. My body began to ache and my legs moved like mechanical stumps. My cheeks were freezing and I began to wonder if this wasn't a foolish thing to be doing after all. *Maybe,* I thought, *maybe it would be better to turn back.* I hesitated in front of a drugstore. *Shoot,* I grunted, *this trip is not worth it.* I started to turn when I seemed to hear my mother saying to me, *"Now Harvey, if you want things in this life, you have to go after them. If you must have help, ask God."*

She used to say things like that to me back in Iowa, where I grew up. When Momma took me to church she'd say, "If you forget everything else you learn here, Harvey, remember that God so loved Harvey Brown that He gave His only begotten Son for him." (That's from John 3:16.) "And whenever you're in trouble, Harvey, repeat the Twenty-third Psalm; it's like medicine."

I looked up. The sun was shining over the buildings, and the cold Chicago air was clear as crystal. I walked on.

The Lord is my shepherd, I shall not want . . .

Yes, I'll get that job.

Like a little fire within me, those words kept me going.

Oops! I slipped again. *Watch those feet.*

By eight o'clock I figured I was over halfway there. Hunching along, I came to a small store, a Hispanic bodega. Its windows were frosted but I knew there was warmth inside. I stumbled through the door, and the savory heat hit me like a blast furnace. I smelled hot coffee.

The owner looked up. "What you doing out on such a cold day?"

"I'm walking to Chicago and Dearborn for a job."

"You crazy, man."

"Yeah, I know," I laughed, "but I need work."

I could stay only a minute, but the warmth revived me. *"Vaya con Dios!"* the owner called as I walked out of the door. *God be with you.*

By the time I hit North Avenue, though, my body seemed a

block of ice; I couldn't feel my mouth anymore. I felt I could not walk any longer.

Lord, help me. I got this far, I've got to make it. Putting one frozen boot before the other, I pushed on.

And then, there was Chicago Avenue. *It's only a little way now.* I pushed a ragged sleeve back from my watch: 9:05. I was late! But then, who else would come out early on a morning like this?

Blinking against the sun, I made out the big YMCA sign ahead. Finally, at 9:10 I pushed through the glass doors. The warm air felt so good that I was tempted to just sit down and rest for a moment, but I walked right up to the service desk. There were already two men ahead of me.

When it finally came my turn to be interviewed, the man at the desk told me, "The job's been filled."

I stared at him.

"Yes, the first man filled the bill and was hired." Then, noticing the look on my face, he said, "I'm sorry, fella."

"Yeah," I sighed, "I am too—after walking seven miles."

His face softened; reaching into his pocket he pulled out a dollar. "Wish I could do more, but this'll get you home." Then he added, "Good luck. With determination like that, you're sure to find something soon."

"Thanks," was all I could manage. In a daze, I walked back out into the cold. As I stood waiting for the bus, I tried to figure it all out. What was the point of this crazy trip anyway?

The bus pulled up and I got on. As it bumped and groaned along Broadway, I stared dully at the sidewalks I had so recently traveled. Where was God, the God Momma said loved Harvey Brown so much? I thought He had been walking with me. Now I wondered.

"Well, Momma," I sighed under my breath, "at least I tried."

Suddenly, I sat up in my seat. I had tried! My long, cold walk hadn't been for nothing. It had made me call out to God for help—and He *had* helped me. He'd given me strength, and He'd given me new determination. Even the man at the YMCA had seen it.

By the time I got home to Emmie, I was feeling pretty good. Somehow I knew that, with God's help, things were going to work out.

Editor's note: *Two weeks later things did work out for Harvey Brown. He got a job with a company taking orders over the phone, using enlarged forms and a desk magnifier to help him read the firm's catalog.*

Part Ten

Pass It On

A Family Time

BY DEVITA CAIN WIDMER
FAYETTEVILLE, NORTH CAROLINA

*Christmas—the one time of year when we
want most of all to belong.*

J ason, our firstborn, was four months old that Christmas
1980. My husband, Steve, was in the Army, stationed in
Bad Aibling, West Germany. It was our third year there,
but the sadness of being away from home seemed worse than
ever.

We'd just come back from a trip to Indiana to see Steve's
father, who was dying, and had introduced Jason to my mom
and dad back in North Carolina. After this time of closeness
with our families, the return to Germany was hard, especially
when word came that Steve's father had died. As Christmas
drew nearer, I could not seem to fight the gloom I felt. Most
of all, I missed the bustling of a large family. I was used to two
turkeys and a ham with all the trimmings, and thirty relatives
packed into one small house on Christmas Day. I wanted my
young son to be part of that, to have those thirty people fussing
over my baby, cuddling him, making him feel welcome and
secure in this world.

Then came a call from Jason's godfather, Don Kraus, who
was stationed at the Army base in Wurzburg. Did we want
company for Christmas? Of course we did! Don arrived two
days before Christmas, bearing gifts, food, and a determination to make the holiday more cheerful for us.

He had a plan for Christmas Eve. We'd drive to a small

291

village in Austria called Oberndorf, where "Silent Night" was composed and first sung on Christmas Eve, 1818. "We'll go to midnight mass," Don said. "It will take several hours to get there. But I promise you it will be worth it."

As we set off that evening, all the world was white and smelled of pine and cedar. We drove in the dark, through the Alps, into Austria, and when we reached Oberndorf, snow was falling lightly. We found a parking place on the cobblestone streets close to the small white church. Villagers were arriving in horse-drawn carts, sleigh bells ringing merrily. Other villagers arrived on foot, strolling arm in arm. People started to enter the church. So did we.

But as we went up the steps, the greeters at the door sadly shook their heads. The church was only large enough to hold members of the congregation and villagers of Oberndorf.

We had traveled all this way to celebrate Christmas in this church, and now we could not even go inside.

The light snow ceased its gentle cascade. It began to grow colder. Steve and Don and I stood in the churchyard as the first strains of music drifted through the doors. Jason began to cry, and I snuggled the baby deeper into the folds of my coat. Now I was crying too. The homesickness, the depression that I'd begun to lose, came back.

There was a scrunch of snow. A silver-haired man approached us, gesturing toward the church door. "Come in, come in," he said. In broken English, he explained that he was one of the elders and we were invited to come in as his guests.

We stepped into the church, filled to overflowing, glowing with candlelight and alive with the sound of caroling. But then, as the music swelled, Jason began to cry. I tried to hush him. He cried even harder. I was embarrassed. Would we continue to be welcome now?

I felt a hand on my arm and turned. A tiny, wizened old woman behind us was reaching out for the baby. I shook my head no, but she leaned over and gently took Jason from me. I watched anxiously as she rocked him in her arms and smiled. Jason stopped crying, and smiled back at her. He seemed contented, so I stopped worrying.

As yet another carol began, I turned and looked again. But Jason was no longer in the old woman's arms!

I gasped. But the woman nodded and gestured across the row. My eyes rapidly scanned the pews. Jason was now several rows away, being passed slowly from one person to the next. As the contented bundle was moved along, I heard whispers explaining, *"Amerikanisches Kind, amerikanisches Kind . . ."*

"Relax," Steve whispered. "Enjoy the service. Jason is fine."

Silent night, holy night . . .

The words filled the sanctuary. With this quiet song of reverence we were welcoming the Christ Child to His world just as surely my own baby was at this moment being welcomed to his. Jason was in the loving arms of a family, a family every bit as real as my own family in America. God's family.

. . . Sleep in heavenly peace . . .

I slipped my arms through Steve's, and he drew me close.

. . . Sleep in heavenly peace.

My Samaritan Experiment

BY JOHN SHERRILL
GUIDEPOSTS CONTRIBUTING EDITOR

I came upon it quite by accident.

One hot afternoon several years ago my wife, Tib, and I were driving along a lonely stretch of I-75 in south Florida when a dashboard warning light began to glow—a red square with a picture of a watering can on it. It was a sign of trouble and I knew I'd have to do something about it. I pulled off on the side of the road and opened the hood.

And that was the beginning of my unexpected adventure—an adventure as a Good Samaritan.

I stared down into the steaming engine. I'm no mechanic, but I could see what the trouble was: The wheel that drives the fan belt had somehow flown apart.

Tib got out too, and we stood in the glare of the August sun, looking down the empty stretch of highway. A car appeared, traveling fast. It passed without slowing down. In a minute or two, another car; that driver didn't even glance at us. I tried to remember what the last big green overhead sign had said. . . . I knew the figure was forty miles. How far had we come since then? Even a few miles would be too far to walk in this heat, and if I tried to drive, the motor would melt.

We stood there on the sun-browned shoulder. A livestock truck went by, then a cluster of cars. No one slowed. Maybe they were afraid to. A rash of highway robberies had recently made headlines in southern Florida. Surely we didn't look dangerous! In any event, we stood beside our automobile as ten, twenty, sixty cars passed. I stopped counting at one hundred.

Finally, an hour and a half later, a muddy pickup slowed as it passed us, turn signal blinking. It pulled onto the shoulder and I ran toward it. The driver, probably in his thirties, wore a yellow cap with the word *Caterpillar* on it. His overalls were caked with gray mud.

"Problemas?" the young farmer asked. He spoke about as much English as I do Spanish, which is to say, not much.

"Cooling system's shot," I said, indicating with a circular gesture that my fan belt wasn't working. The man walked back to our car, looked under the hood and shook his head. With sign language—pointing to us, then to his truck, extending both arms as if steering a wheel—he told us clearly enough that he'd take us to find help. So we locked the car and got into the cab of the truck. To see out the mud-splattered windshield from my spot in the middle, I had to look past a crucifix dangling from the mirror.

The farmer took the first exit, twenty miles down the road. It was another five miles to the nearest town. At the garage he waited long enough to be sure we were being looked after, then headed for his truck. I followed, pulling out my wallet in an awkward offer to pay him for his trouble. He shook his head no. So we simply shook hands, and he was gone.

It took the garage several hours to locate a suitable part, but before nightfall we were on our way, still giving thanks for our Good Samaritan. "How do you repay a kindness like that?" I said to Tib.

"We can't," she said, "but maybe we can pass it along."

Pass it along! Of course—there was my answer. "I'm going to do it," I said to Tib. "I'm going to stop and help another driver stuck on a highway somewhere." I paused. That seemed so little. "No, not *one* other driver," I said. "I'm going to help ten!"

Forming that high-minded resolve was one thing; acting on it was another. The very next day after our Good Samaritan experience we saw a stalled car and I slowed down—until I spotted the man inside wearing studded black leather. I kept going. I probably misjudged the poor guy, but still . . . there *are* angry and deranged people out there. Clearly there had to be a certain rightness about stopping. That's a judgment call, so I'd ask God to guide me.

Then too, like most people I always seem to be in a hurry. The next few times I saw a car stopped beside the road, it happened that someone was waiting for me at the other end, so again I did not stop. Perhaps it was just an excuse, but is it fair, after all, to do a good deed at the expense of someone else?

After that bumbling false start, however, I did find plenty of occasions when I could assist someone. Tib's and my work as writers keeps us on the move.

Tib was with me on my very first Samaritan adventure. We were driving through rural New Jersey when we passed a late-model Lincoln stopped beside the road, with a family gathered around it—a man, a woman and two youngsters. Both the father and the little boy were wearing yarmulkes.

Tib and I exchanged nods.

The embarrassed man told us they'd run out of gas. We opened the back door and the father got in. As we drove to the nearest filling station we told him the story of the Good Samaritan who had stopped for us in Florida.

That night, Tib and I were unpacking the car back home in New York when on the floor of the back seat we found a wallet.

Inside was the identification of the man we had stopped for, an anesthesiologist from Trenton. I reached him by phone and told him I'd sent it by certified mail in the morning.

"I hope you weren't worried," I added.

"Of course not. Would the Good Samaritan steal?"

Since then I have stopped for breakdowns in half a dozen states, as well as in Canada, Mexico, and Europe.

Being a Good Samaritan has sometimes involved more than just a helping hand. Sometimes it has required a small expense—a couple of dollars for phone calls, or a cup of coffee. One day I was driving through the outskirts of Charleston, South Carolina, when I passed a truck filled with fresh produce, stalled at curbside with its hood raised. A block farther I noticed a grizzled man trudging down the road, lugging what looked like a heavy auto part. I pulled over. "That your truck back there?"

The stubble-bearded man put down his load. "This confounded starter motor again! If you can take me to the parts yard . . ."

As it turned out, the man was just a few dollars short of the price of the replacement part. A very few—nothing like the size of the smile that warmed me on my way after I'd driven the man back to his truck.

Sometimes stopping has cost me more time than anticipated. Barreling along a California freeway one winter day I passed an old Pinto on the edge of the highway, flying the universal signal of distress: a handkerchief tied to the radio antenna. A woman sat in the driver's seat.

By the time I'd reacted to the situation, I was perhaps a quarter mile past her, with no place to pull over. I'd have to exit, reverse direction and get off again in order to get back to her. The round trip took twenty minutes, during which time I was sure someone else would have stopped. But no, the woman was still there, and she was crying.

"Don't mind me," she apologized. "I've been sitting here over an hour. Even the police didn't stop."

I took extra time with her, driving her to a restaurant and waiting until the road-service people arrived. Over coffee I told her about our Florida experience. "Thank God for that farmer," she said as the tow truck pulled in. "Because of him you stopped today."

It's true. Because of that farmer, a minor chain reaction of kindness has started. About three months after this adventure began, Tib and I were driving along a levee above the Mississippi River when we came upon a young black woman in a battered station wagon full of children. We pulled alongside and asked if she was having car trouble.

Indeed she was. They'd stopped to eat a picnic lunch and now her car wouldn't start. With our jumper cables I got her engine going. "How much?" she asked, opening a worn brown handbag. In answer I told her about the farmer who had stopped for us.

"I'm going to do it!" she exclaimed. "I'm going to help out ten people just like you're doing!"

This young mother's reaction to my story of the Florida Samaritan was typical. People often promised to pass thoughtfulness along. Some admitted they'd be too timid to stop along a highway, but they said they'd find some other way to help, such as calling the highway patrol at the next exit.

I am glad others want to keep the Samaritan chain intact. They may find, as I have, that the rewards far outweigh the help given to a stranger. Some responses are touching. One skinny boy with a huge radio, which he kept at full volume throughout our drive to a motorcycle shop, shouted that he couldn't believe someone old enough to be his *father* had stopped to help him.

But for me the biggest reward has been a shift in my own attitudes. Over the years I had slowly become a bit suspicious of people who are not my neighbors—people from another race, another generation or culture. It's well to be sensible, of course; we do live in a century of violence (as did the biblical Good Samaritan). But I am not going to let fear play a larger-than-life role for me. Most people are friendly, most are honest, and I want to side with those who say that this is true—like the Samaritan in the dirt-splattered pickup who stopped to help us.

It has been more than three years since I pulled over for my first motorist-in-need. During this time I've met tourists from Japan, businessmen, a rodeo clown, several students, a Jamaican migrant worker. My tenth stop has long since been completed. But by now I am enjoying these encounters so much that I wouldn't stop stopping for the world!

Basic Training

BY VICKIE ALDOUS
SALMON, IDAHO
SENIOR, SALMON HIGH SCHOOL

*And to think I actually chose this for
my summer vacation!*

I had never felt farther from God in my whole life.

It was Sunday morning, and as the lights flooded the barracks for wake-up, my only wish was to be back home safely in bed.

How did I ever get into this? I asked myself as I crawled from beneath my woolen blanket. I wondered if any of the other fifty girls in my platoon were as tired as I was.

I remembered my junior year in high school and my first visit with the Army recruiter. He told me how I could join the Reserves and earn money to help pay for college. All I had to do was complete two months of basic training in the summer between eleventh and twelfth grades. When I graduated from high school, I would spend another summer in advanced training, and then serve weekend drills in my home state.

It seemed perfect. How hard could two months of basic be? I knew I could survive anything for that length of time.

Now, as I made my bed with perfect, squared corners, I wasn't so sure.

I had always considered myself physically fit, but the Army's idea of physically fit was entirely different. Each day we got up at 4:00 A.M. to exercise. The routines alternated: One morning we did sit-ups and push-ups for an hour, and the next we ran anywhere from three to four and a half miles. This was called P.T., "physical training." To me, the initials meant "prolonged torture."

I had run cross-country and track in high school, so the run was not too difficult for me. The sit-ups and push-ups were something else, though. Only a week into basic I was so sore that I could barely move. My shoulders cramped from activities as simple as lifting a fork during chow. Whenever I laughed, which wasn't often, my stomach muscles ached.

Often during the predawn darkness of P.T., I looked up at the stars from the sit-up position and wondered if there really was a God up there. Had He forsaken me?

None of us were used to being yelled at by drill sergeants night and day for anything, no matter how trivial, done wrong. Many were away from home for the first time. There was virtually no privacy, and we received, on average, about five hours of sleep each night.

The biggest taboo of all was to break down and cry. The few people who had allowed tears to fall were branded as crybabies.

We were constantly on edge and irritated with one another. I had always got along fairly well with people and rarely lost my temper. But now I found myself restraining an impulse to strangle people.

Our drill sergeants could plainly see our lack of camaraderie and they used it against us. Whenever an individual made a mistake, we all paid. Dropping and doing push-ups because someone twitched at the wrong moment did not exactly endear that person to the platoon.

Of course, the Army had its own logic for this system. It fostered peer pressure to always do the right thing, even when the drill sergeant's back was turned. Everybody was pitted against everybody else. We became our own police force.

This morning was no different, even if it was Sunday. It was supposed to be our day off, but the reality was something else. We had to scrub the barracks spotlessly clean from top to bottom. In addition, every Sunday our platoon was charged with mowing and raking an area of lawn as large as a football field.

As I got dressed, I noticed that the fighting and bickering were already under way. People were arguing over who would get the morning shifts for lawn detail. It was better to do it in the relative cool of morning than wait and be out working under the blazing afternoon summer sun.

I went around the squabbling groups and put my name on the afternoon list. I wanted to go to church that morning. Devotion to God wasn't my only reason. I just didn't feel like fighting my way through all those people. Also, this was about my only chance for some peace and quiet, and I intended to take advantage of it.

The church was filled to its capacity of about 400 people. I sat in a pew with about ten other girls from my platoon, and we all listened politely as the sermon began. The chaplain wasn't very enthusiastic. It was his fourth service of the morning, and he was probably worn out. His subject was generic— about keeping God in sight when faced with adversity. Instead of inspiring me, it only emphasized my feelings of isolation. I felt all alone, even though I was surrounded by Christians. Why couldn't God show me He still loved me—now when I needed Him most?

The chaplain's message ended and he asked if anyone had anything to share. We all sat in silence, until a girl stood up.

"I would like to sing a song I wrote," she said nervously.

I was surprised. Nothing would have convinced me to talk

in front of all those people, let alone sing. I admired her for it.

Her first simple words went straight to my heart:

God, I'm feeling so alone
in this place so far from home.
Please listen to this prayer
and show me You still care.

Here was someone going through the same thing I was! Her words were sure and beautiful now as she went on with the song, and every verse echoed my own secret thoughts. Now I knew I wasn't the only one who felt so isolated, but I still couldn't understand how God could have abandoned us.

Suddenly I was overwhelmed with self-pity, and tears welled up in my eyes. *Dear God,* I prayed, *please don't let me cry in front of all these people!*

I glanced around furtively to see if anyone had noticed. To my surprise, everybody around me was fighting back tears too! I looked up and didn't even bother to wipe my tears away. "Hey, you guys," I whispered, "we're *not* alone. We have one another."

For a few seconds, we looked around dazedly as the realization slowly dawned on us. It was as if we all were looking beyond the tough outsides and fighting to see the potential friends in front of us. We had been so busy trying to hide our feelings, we didn't even realize others felt the same way.

God hadn't abandoned us. Far from it! He had actually provided us with many people for help and support. He knew we didn't need someone to carry us through basic, we needed Someone to give us the strength and confidence to make it on our own, and friends to encourage us along the way.

That's when we all broke down. Everyone was hugging one another, smiling and crying at the same time.

Then the girl who had started all this finished her song:

How could I have been so blind?

Why'd it take so long to find?

Your love's before my eyes,

in the friends that You supply.

As she sat down, the rest of us stood up, clapping. All around our small group, row by row, people got to their feet. Soon the whole church was giving her a standing ovation.

With a simple song, God had shown us that He was still there, and He loved us.

Maybe it wasn't so simple after all.